CW00470506

TURNING THE AIR
BLUE

A barrage of the funniest, rudest, cheekiest yells, chants,
shouts and comments which have turned the air blue at
Goodison over the years. Compiled by bluekipper.com

The Bluecoat Press

© www.bluekipper.com 2005

Published by The Bluecoat Press, Liverpool
Compiled by www.bluekipper.com
Book design by March Graphic Design Studio, Liverpool
Printed by Graham & Heslip

ISBN 1 904438 25 3

All rights reserved. No part of this publication may be reproduced, stored in a retrieval system, or transmitted in any form or by any means, electronic, mechanical, photocopying, recording or otherwise, without prior permission from the publisher.

ACKNOWLEDGEMENTS We would like to thank the following for their help with the book and the web site www.bluekipper.com Sting Ray, Mickey Blue Eyes, Roy Caine, Mark Flynn, Sunlink, Sower of the Seed, Ian Mills for help with the photos, the message board admin team, Paul Mac, Nikkie, Blue Q, Thommo, Hoogie, Geraghty, Moff for the cheese, Bod, Big Ted, Father Ted, Hamble, Po, Pootle, Selwyn Froggett, Les The Lab Technician, Jerry St Clair, Richard Nixon, Glen Keeley, Glenn Campbell, Alistair Campbell, Alistair Sim, Joan Simms, Joan Collins, Roger Melly, Terry Waite's Allotment, and all Evertonians around the world. You know you are the best.

CONTENTS

FOREWORD

I HAVE HAD THE MISFORTUNE of meeting the lads from www.bluekipper.com too many times over the last couple of years. However, after I realised it was through coincidence rather than a preplanned stalking activity, I came to appreciate that they are just typical lunatic Evertonians like all of us. They love a good laugh and love Everton Football Club more than anything else.

As a Scouser and an Evertonian, I can appreciate the humour behind 'most' of the shouts and admit that a lot of the shouts helped me to enjoy my career even more.

The collection of shouts they have put together typify those I heard every week playing for the Blues. Yes, you can hear individual shouts out of 40,000 voices, especially if they are directed personally at you.

In particular, I remember arriving at Goodison on match-day a couple of years ago and being met by the usual autograph hunters. One of the lads pointed me out to a young kid saying, "That's Dave Watson, he used to wear the armband for Everton." The kid replied, "Why? Can't he swim?" Fantastic.

I wish the lads the best of luck with this book and continuing good fortune with the website in the future. Hopefully they will now leave me alone and stop pestering me with pieces of cheese.

Dave Watson

INTRODUCTION

ON A BALMY SUMMER'S EVENING in June 2000, five Evertonians who had been mates for over 25 years met up in Doctor Duncan's pub in the centre of Liverpool. It was here, in an alcoholic haze, where the idea of www.bluekipper.com was born. As the night wore on and the beer flowed more freely, so did the suggestions of content for the site.

One of the suggestions came from Sausage, who like many other Toffees was introduced to the Everton religion by his Dad, or, as many of us fondly refer to Dads as, "me arl fella". Sausage was mesmerised as a kid when his Dad used to bellow out at the game and longed for the day when he could do the same.

His early recollection is whenever a player went down injured his arl fella would shout, "Give him a Double Diamond – it works wonders!" This was the punchline in the beer advert at the time. And so the 'Me Arl Fella's Shouts' section on our website was born. Since then we have been sent over 600 shouts and compiled them here for your enjoyment.

Thanks

Kipper, Jogger, Keefer, Lard, Lavo and Sausage.

THEY MUST LOVE COMING TO GOODISON

THE EDUCATED GOODISON CROWD has long been acknowledged for appreciating good play by the visiting team. However, if the play is not good, or the player is not liked, then don't hold back ...

THE FUNNIEST I heard was at a match v Arsenal in '78. Arsenal's famous full back (now on the backroom staff) came to take a throw-in at the Bullens Road. A Scouser shouted, "Rice! You're nothin' but a Puddin'." Even Pat himself saw the funny side. We won 2-1, so I was laughing all the way home. Two goals from Big Bob! **Jay, Warrington (06/09/04)**

EVERTON v FOREST yonks ago. Half-time it was when Tony Woodcock came out to a great cheer from the Forest fans. The linesman was waiting to introduce him to the game. When some scally shouted, "Oi! Woodcock! Does yer tart get splinters?" The girls in front of us were laughing their heads off at that. Woodcock just shook his head in disgust. The Everton bench all burst out laughing. **Carl Dutton (17/09/04)**

AT COLIN HARVEY'S testimonial, everyone was taking the piss out of Bologna's Smit, singing, "You're Smit and you know you are." My girlfriend asks who Smit is, so I point him out. Guy in row behind points at Alexandersson and says, "You see that blonde? He's smit as well!" **Eli (03/09/03)**

GREATEST SHOUT I have ever heard – Bellamy for the umpteenth time moaning at the referee, a bloke behind me in the Street End stands up and shouts, "Oi! Bellamy! Fuck off back to Lord of the Rings will ya?" Quality. Everyone in our area of the stand was rolling about laughing! Shortly after you could hear some people explaining to the slow ones, "Bellamy looks like a Hobbit." Quality. **Ted (28/07/03)**

AT THE BORO GAME this year and some wag shouted to Ray Parlour, "Put a fuckin bra on Charlie Dimmock!" The whole of the Paddock was in stitches. **Get your hair cut (20/11/04)**

IN THE RECENT HOME GAME against Southampton (after the home game v Spurs), the Upper Bullens was quiet, when a wag who sits behind me jumped up out of his seat and cried out, "I fuckin' hate you, Redknapp". The whole of my area started pissing ourselves laughing. He was only a week late! **Duncans Pigeon (08/11/04)**

ME AND MY ARL FELLA were at the Sunderland game sitting in the lower Gwladys Street, when Mr Rennie gave another strange decision. My arl fella jumped up and shouted, "You're fucking shite, ref. You're the only Rennie I know that gives people heart burn." Priceless moment. **Dave Tomo (10/02/05)**

LATE SEVENTIES, HOME TO MIDDLESBROUGH during the dark days of Gordon (is a moron) Lee. David Mills (founder member of the Ugly Squad) goes to take a corner at the Street End. A shout goes up, "Oi! Mills! Take that fuckin' mask off, der's kids 'round 'ere!" Street End collapses in laughter and even Mills had a smile (I think that's what it was) on his ... er ... face. **Frank Boyle (24/09/03)**

YEARS AGO US versus The Arse, Charlie Nicholas was out warming up with the rest of The Arse and decides to head toward the Gladders. Charlie being the great player he was, was absolutely astonished to hear us Blues singing his name, "Charlie Nicholas ... Charlie Nicholas ... Charlie Nicholas ..." and just as he puts his hand up to clap us in appreciation, the whole of the Gladders in union, pipes up, "... is a wanker ... is a wanker." Total classic, his face and dejection were a sight to behold. **Bally (02/10/04)**

SEASON BEFORE LAST at the Birmingham game Robbie Savage comes near us in the Bullens to take a throw-in. The lad behind me who is always funny shouts, "Oi! Lily! Les Dawson was better than you on Blanketty Blank." He went bright red and we were all in fits. **Ludo (24/08/04)**

AGAINST BLACKBURN AT HOME, Rooney was running the show in the first half, when ex-Kopite David Thompson tried and failed to clatter him. On his third attempt a shout from the back of the Gwladys Street terrace was heard, "Fuck off back to Dr Zeus, you fucking chimp." The stand erupted into laughter. Shortly after this, as Thompson was taking a corner, a young boy was spotted in the corner doing an impression of a chimpanzee, which to his eternal credit even Thompson found funny! The fact that the said boy looked more like a mental patient may have had something to do with it! A good laugh was had by all! **Ted (06/02/03)**

ME AND ME MATES were at the Everton Middlesbrough game this season and we couldn't stop laughin' as some fella in the Gwladys shouts, "Maccarone, you cheesy twat." **Graeme Beresford (18/11/02)**

GOING BACK TO 1966/67. In a match against Man City Mike Summerbee responded to chants about, "Lee bums Bell, Bell bums Lee, Lee and Bell bums Summerbee ... (to the tune of 'This Old Man') and he trotted away from the Street End showing his arse. **Janet and Gerry (31/10/02)**

LEICESTER LAST YEAR sitting in the Park End some bloke shouts to their goalie, "Eh! Walker! Is yer dad still on the dole?" We all crack up, but Walker turned round laughing and nods. Good on him. But then the bloke shouts back, "Well, fuck off and get yer hair cut. You scruffy twat!" Brilliant. **Gary Dunne (21/05/03)**

AT THE ARSENAL GAME in the Gwladys and Thierry Henry comes over to take a corner. As soon as he reaches the corner flag about 40 of us stand up and start singing, "yer can stick yer Va Va Voom up yer arse." Kept us laughing for ages. **Mark 'Earl' Barrett (13/01/04)**

AT THE SOUTHAMPTON MATCH this season, the Saints defender Jelle Van Damme came to take a throw-in near the Paddock. As he walks over, he looks to where I'm sitting and the fella behind me shouts, "an' ya films are shite too!" **Chris Sillett (20/11/04)**

ABOUT TWO YEARS AGO we were watching Everton play Man U in the Paddock at Goodison. After a foul by Unsworth on Beckham, Beckham's shorts were pulled up slightly. After a bit of abuse, he pulled his shorts up a bit more and showed us his arse cheek! A fella behind me replied with, "It's not as spotty as ya bird's face." Sir David wasn't smiling then! **Spinksy (09/01/04)**

I WAS SITTING in the Park End last season against Birmingham, and Birmingham went on the attack only for the Stern John to fire a shot wide. As he walked away from a shite effort on goal, some old fella in the Park End piped up with, "Fuck off you, Stern John, with yer name arse end about!" Myself and everyone around was in stitches. **Johnny Bri (20/11/03)**

AT THE MINI DERBY last season at Halton – Marcus Babbel had just butted Chaddy and was sent off. He walked right past the Everton crowd and one dad shouted, "Auf Wiedersehen, Dumbkopf." Babbel wasn't impressed and mouthed some sort of German response, but one young fan shouted, "Yeah – off with his head!" **Steve (17/11/03)**

AT THE EVERTON v NEWCASTLE game this season, Shearer was being his usual cheating self, backing into Yobo. Some fella behind me in the top balcony stands up and shouts, "Ding ding ding. Two pound ninety-nine. Fuck off, Shearer, you fuckin' barcode." **Hughesy (19/10/03)**

HEARD IN THE PADDOCK V BIRMINGHAM on Wednesday night directed towards Savage. "If you were fined ten thousand pound for havin' a shit, how much was yer ma fined for havin' you?" **Tommy Malone (04/09/02)**

A FEW YEARS AGO playing Wimbledon at Goodison. It was bloody freezing and about 300 Blues are queuing up for some tickets when Sam Hamman and two minders walk past pointing at the queue and laughing hysterically, warm as toast in bad sheepies and leathers. One lad shouts from the back, "What the fuck are you laughin' at, yer tin pot? It's called a queue!" **SmnPil (04/09/02)**

AGAINST MAN UTD at home, Veron was about to take a corner and the fella in front of me shouted, "Sort yer economy out, Veron and fuck off." **Foy (30/12/01)**

A COUPLE OF SEASONS ago we were playing Spurs, and after a pretty hard tackle from Rhino on Ginola, the Frenchman gets up and starts complaining to the ref. A woman from behind me shouts, "That was just a bit of British beef, you French tart." **Duggy (24/12/01)**

THE BEST ONE I heard was from the Street End when Cantona had just come back after the infamous palace game. Somebody shouted, "Jump in 'ere and see if you can get back out, yer twat." **Gary Killen (31/10/01)**

THERE'S A GUY in the Gwladys that shouted at a keeper with a colourful shirt on, "Oi, keeper – you look like an accident in a felt tip factory!" **Hoogie (26/09/01)**

A FEW YEARS BACK against Spurs when Klinnsman was playing for them and he had gone to ground once too often, some old wag behind me shouted, "That twat's up and down more times than Princess Margaret's knickers." **Sean O'Flynn (22/09/01)**

MAN U MONDAY NIGHT. As Forlan was waiting to come on one of the lads shouted, "Here's fuckin' Sally Gunnell on steroids." Caused a right scream all around us. Sat behind us was the legend who is Duncan McKenzie and even he laughed. **Fredsnotred (10/10/02)**

13

A FEW YEARS AGO when we were playing Chelsea at Goodison, around the time Dennis Wise got convicted of punching a taxi driver in London. Wise was having a nondescript game, and came over to take a corner by the Gwladys Street End. As he put the ball on the spot, a fella a few seats from me shouted, "Taxi for Wise! Taxi for Wise!" **Stephen Lyon (31/07/02)**

MIDDLE OF THE FIRST HALF, already 1-0 down against Chelsea a couple of weeks back – Chelsea subs start warming up in front of us – Dalla Bonehead runs by, very self-consciously running his fingers through his shiny golden blonde locks – to be met with, "Two coffees, and a tea please, luv!" We all broke up including Alec Cleland running behind him (some things never change). **John Collins (03/05/02)**

A FEW SEASONS AGO, during another boring home game, the rather large scooter Micky Quinn was warming up on the touch line by doing press-ups against the advertising hoardings, when in front of us, in the Lower Street End, a supporter looked up from reading his paper and shouted, "Aye! Fat arse! You'll fuckin' break that." Brilliant. **Brian Campion (12/04/02)**

AT THE GAME against Middlesbrough a few years back, Ravenelli started giving the referee verbals for not getting a free kick, when this guy behind me shouts, "Fuck off you, Tom O'Connor." Class. **Gary Holmes (06/04/02)**

AT THE LEEDS MATCH. That fair player, David Batty, went for a ball Kung Fu-style and studded Scott Gemmill in the chest. Fella behind shouts, "Fuck off, Batty. Who do yer think you are? Billy Elliot?" **Anon (04/03/02)**

HEARD AT THE RECENT Ipswich home game as Mark Venus bent over to place the ball for a corner, "Hey! Venus! We can see Uranus." **Bob Thomason (16/02/02)**

IN THE BIRMINGHAM GAME Mario Melchiot come over to take a throw and my mate shouted, "Fuck off! Scritti Politti!" We were all a bit puzzled until he went, "Err, I mean Milli Vannili!" Crazy, everyone was in bulk. **Blue Hawaii (30/11/04)**

EXCLUSIVE ALEX YOUNG INTERVIEW

WHAT A BIRTHDAY PRESENT! Blue Kipper were privileged to be given half an hour with the Golden Vision on 12 August 2001, our first birthday. It happened in The Adelphi Hotel, whilst Alex was doing a signing session, before his testimonial dinner later that night.

It was a great honour for me to meet Alex Young in person, as he is a living legend and besides Dixie Dean, is Everton's most famous player. You can imagine what it was like for me to walk into a room and be met by the Golden Vision. I need not have worried, he was friendly straight from the start and put me at ease immediately.

I joined Alex during a signing session for Bigbluetube and he had just started to sign 500 copies of a photographic print of himself scoring a goal at Blackburn in 1961 – his first goal for Everton. After a break for tea and sandwiches, I had 20 minutes with Alex whilst he continued the signing.

BK: You were called 'The Blonde Bombshell' at Hearts and 'Golden Vision' at Everton, which do you prefer?

AY: I think 'Golden Vision' was always my favourite.

"Keep signing Alex," a voice in the back shouted, because Alex had stopped what he was doing to think about the question.

BK: Which was the best player you played with at Everton?

AY: It's very difficult to pick out just one. It's either Bally, Vernon, Tony Kay, or Bobby Collins, these four would be my choice.

BK: If you had to pick just one, Alex, who would it be?

He took a deep breath and stopped signing again.

AY: It would maybe be Bally. But there were other great players: Colin Harvey, a classy player in that era, and Howard Kendall too. There is not much difference between those players, but Bally just shades it!

BK: What about players in the Scotland team? Who was the greatest you lined up with?

AY: Dave Mackay (he said without hesitation).

BK: Who was the best opponent you played against?

AY: I remember playing against Duncan Edwards, for one game only. I was playing for the Scottish U-23 team. The match was played in Sheffield, I was just eighteen and playing number eight. He was number six. He was awesome, a real powerhouse of a player.

BK: What do you remember about the only match you played for Scotland against England?

AY: It was at Hampden and ended 1-1. I played number eight, Ian St John was number nine. Dennis Law was number ten. But I didn't really get involved for the majority of the game and the match really passed me by. I could have done much better. I had just a couple of touches but I could have played ten times better. For those kind of matches you need to get pumped up a bit and they never had a coach or a manager to get us going. Besides that, I know Scotland should have won it by a mile! St John was clean through three times straight down the middle, one-on-one with the goalie each time, and he missed all three. So I blamed Ian! It was very disappointing to come off after a game, and you never performed as a player.

BK: You played in all forty-two games during the Championship-winning season 1962/63, which is some feat. Did you ever play with injuries?

AY: I played with knocks, but I never suffered from pulls or strains. Many players today are troubled by pulled muscles but I was lucky never to suffer from that. Footballers today are not namby pamby, or anything like that, I just think they are more prone to injury, with training from a younger age.

BK: What would you say was your greatest achievement as a player?

AY: Maybe winning all the trophies that could be won in Scotland and then winning all the trophies that could be won in England, at the time, anyhow. The League and Cup at Hearts, in Scotland, and both the League and Cup with Everton.

BK: If you had to pick the League or Cup, which would you pick?

AY: It would have to be the League, as it's the best team which wins the League, it's not always the best team which wins the Cup. It was a big thrill to win the Cup, but to win the League! Oh! We ran away with the League that year. In the end I think we finished thirteen points clear. Everton had not won the League for a long time, so it meant a lot to the fans. The same with Hearts. When we won the Scottish League, in 1957, we hadn't won the League for sixty years. So yes, to win the four medals from both countries is special.

BK: When you came down from Hearts to Everton, did you find it hard to adjust?

AY: No, not at all. When I came down I had a back splint on my leg. I didn't play at all for about two months and then it took

18

about another two months to get fit. The move was no trouble
and I felt at home right away. There were good players near
me. Roy Vernon and Bobby Collins for example.

BK: What about coming from Edinburgh to Merseyside?

AY: The same: I felt at home immediately. Even though I hadn't
played, there was no pressure to hurry me along and get me
in the starting team and they just waited for me to get better.
Goodison is very special and it soon became my home from
home.

BK: Looking back to the Cup Final of 1966, was it a penalty?

AY: Aye, Guaranteed. He definitely pulled my standing foot away.
The referee was behind.

BK: In the same match, you scored, but the goal was disallowed
for offside. Can you remember it?

AY: Yes, although I still can't understand why it was offside as I
had run on to the ball from a deep position, through a couple
of players.

BK: What did you do after the match?

AY: We went to the Waldorf, I think, where we had a big dinner
with all the team and our wives.

BK: Any high jinks?

AY: No. It was a brilliant dinner, but we just enjoyed ourselves.

BK: You have mentioned Alan Ball as one of the best players you
played with at Everton. How did you get on with him?

AY: We roomed together for a year and a half until Harry really
put the knife in and split us up. I always got on well with Bally.
He had seen me play before he joined Everton and said he
would love to play in the same side as me. I knew Alan's
game and I thought he could play. We became friends and
would go racing together.

BK: You bought a horse together didn't you?

AY: Aye, yes we did, we only had it for one season. We bought it for thirteen thousand guineas. The horse was well bred and it ran four times as a two-year-old. We had it for a year and then sold it for eighty quid, not forgetting all the training fees we'd spent. It was one of the first horses for Barry Hills the trainer. That was his first season but he went on to be a champion trainer and widely respected. The horse had no pace, but it was well bred. We thought it was going to be a cracker. In the same year Labby saw a horse in a field over on the Wirral and decided to buy it. It was a thoroughbred and he had ten winners!

BK: What do you think of the loyalty of players to the clubs today? In particular, what do you think of Frannie Jeffers and now Michael Ball leaving Everton?

AY: I'm surprised the two of them left. I don't want to criticise the young players. When we were at a club, you couldn't just walk away, you had to just do as you were told and play as well as you could. But nowadays it seems you can just walk away. I don't know, there seems to be a lot of money about and it seems that Everton need the money.

BK: It seems like it has turned around a bit, with the likes of you and Bally and others who never wanted to go?

AY: Bally was transferred but he didn't want to go. Bobby Collins didn't want to go either. I'm sorry to see both Ball and Jeffers go. I think if the money from SKY was taken away, the clubs couldn't pay the wages they have agreed to pay and there would be a problem then.

BK: My first game at Goodison was the last game of the 1963 Championship season against Fulham. I don't remember much about the game, do you?

AY: Taffy Vernon scored three, I scored none. I was leading scorer up until that game, and Taffy beat me by one goal.

BK: What about the characters in the team?

AY: Fellows like Westy – he was a character – a funny lad. Brian
        Harris was a piss-taker. Bally never shut up. Ernie Hunt was
        also a funny lad, he came from Coventry. He was always
        driving around with a gorilla mask on! He had a false arm,
        which was very hairy. He'd ask someone a question on the
        street and then shake hands with them to thank them and then
        laugh at their reaction.

BK: I know it's a silly question, but are you looking forward to the
        match tomorrow? (Everton 1 – 0 Espanyol, 13 August 2001)

AY: Oh! Aye! It's great for me and for the Foundation. I'm chuffed
        about it, I didn't want all the money myself, sharing it with the
        Foundation is great. It means other former players who need
        help will receive something and that is a great thing. Hopefully
        everyone enjoys the day. I'm sure it will be a nice day with a
        smashing crowd. It came as a great surprise when they told
        me it was going to happen. So yes, I'm really looking forward
        to it.

FROM THE MOUTHS ...

THE INNOCENCE OF YOUTH gives us some great shouts. Fortunately, some of the not so innocent young Toffees come up with some classics as well.

WELL MY FAMILY is from Scunthorpe (2 hours east) and it was Everton v Fulham and we took my little brother with us for the first time and he's 6 years old. We were outside the ground and the usual banter between people was going on and my brother comes out with, "What language do these people speak?" Everyone around us cracked up. Classic. **Danny Aitken (Sunny Scunny) (28/07/03)**

SPURS AT HOME a few seasons ago, when Ginola was diving for them. Ginola had ambled into the box and dived, when a fella in the Lower Gwladys jumps up and shouts, "Get up, you dirty diving French bastard," followed by his young daughter shouting, "Dad, sit down. You're embarrassing me." **Andy Irving (24/09/03)**

MAN UTD ON SATURDAY, 3-0 down, I headed for a slash. The bogs were chocka but no one spoke, until this little lad piped up, "Dad ... if they score another one, I'm gonna go mad." Cue uproar. Brilliant. **Si (13/02/04)**

I'M A LIFE-LONG EVERTONIAN and season ticket holder. Last season my 9-year-old cousin started coming with us every game without fail. When all goes silent he will stand up and shout at the top of his voice, "The referees a banker." Has everyone in the lower Gwladys by us in stitches. **Mikey McD Robbo (17/07/03)**

A COUPLE OF YEARS AGO in Joe Parky's testimonial against City, Mark (Kopite) Kennedy came to take a corner at the Gwladys Street. Some goofy-lookin' lad about 7 just came running down at him and screamed, "Fuck off, Kennedy, you prostitute!" The youth of today, eh? **Peter Nesbo (13/01/04)**

AFTER THE CHELSEA GAME the other week, mingling with them by the Park End after the match. The 'Sign on, sign on' song went off by the Cockney geezers and this little Blue, about 10 years old, shouted, "Go on! Fuck off back to your mansions!" **Eddie Bramhill (20/12/03)**

EVERTON v ARSENAL. Jeffers warming up on the touchline taking merciless barracking from the Park End. After a while it quietened down and the little voice of the 8-year-old kid in front of me in the family enclosure shouts, "Can you move your ears please, Franny? I can't see the match!" Hilarity ensued. **Flipper (24/10/02)**

HOME GAME AGAINST FULHAM first half and Li Tie is brought down. Some slight pushing results in a small kid nearby shouting at the top of his voice, "Give him a Chinese burn." **Joe Cody (10/10/02)**

AT A YOUTH MATCH four years ago, a kid in the main stand was talking to his mate about Danny Cadamarteri, his new hair cut and how his form had dipped. He said, "He's never been the same since he had his padlocks cut off!" Classic. **Blue4ever (15/05/02)**

MAN AND FIVE-YEAR-OLD LAD. Player lies on the pitch awaiting treatment. "Dad, is he dead?" **Paul (14/01/02)**

PLAYING THE HAMMERS one year, Ian Dowie got booked for absolutely nothing. A small kid in front of me said to his dad, "Why has he been booked, Dad?" To which someone else replied, "Cos he's fucking ugly." Classic. **Neil (16/02/02)**

A FEW YEARS AGO I was at the Chelsea game when Duncan won us a penalty and the keeper was sent off! I was sitting in the Family Enclosure near the corner flag when Scott Minto came over to take a corner. A young lad of about 14 shouted, "Minto, yer minty get!" Minto was totally confused as to what it meant. Classic. **Lou (02/04/02)**

LAST SEASON, think it was the Villa game. Ferguson had just come on and flapped in front of goal, much to the dismay of the Lacoste-clad kidda next to me, who shouted, "Fuck off, Ferguson. You've done nothin' this year, apart from fight crime!" **The Jiggerrabbit (26/07/03)**

LUTON TOWN SEMI at Villa. Ref makes some stupid decision and me mate stands up to hurl abuse but spots this Dad with his three small lads next to him. Mindful of his language he shouts, "Ref, yer ... narner!" Ten-year-old scall turns to his Dad and says, "Dad, that stupid twat just called the ref a narner." **Gratistuta (21/10/02)**

MY FIRST MATCH

NO MATTER HOW OLD YOU WERE, or how long ago it was, everyone remembers their first visit to Paradise like it was yesterday.

WHEN I SIGNED on to Blue Kipper you asked me to tell you about my first Everton game and, believe me, at my age, that's a hard one to answer. The first trip to God's Country was with me Dad to see the reserves playing Bury reserves. We won 2-0 so that was me pointed in the right direction for the rest of my life. As much as I've tried I can't remember the first big game that I went to, but I'll try to recollect some memories. I was in the boy's pen for a Cup-tie against Spurs and we won on an Eddie Wainwright penalty. I remember the great TG Jones calmly heading the ball back to Ted Sagar against Stoke City. The only thing was, Sagar was coming for the ball and it ended up an OG. The crowd went deathly quiet and I'm sure I heard Sagar say, "Hey, Tommy, try not to do that again," or words to that effect.

I recall sagging school on a Wednesday afternoon to see a Cup replay against Leyton Orient (we drew 1-1 down there) and we got battered 3-1. I also sagged school to see us hammer Brentford 6-1. That was when we scored 20 goals in three games! Derby 6-2, Brentford and then Plymouth 8-4. Millions of memories come to mind when you get down to thinking about them and I wouldn't swap one of them (even the bad ones). But if you can bear with me, I would like to relate the best of them. Everton versus Man United in the Cup (early 50s?) They had Cockburn, Carey, Chilton, Rowley, Mitten, etc – a great team. BUT we had the greatest man that ever wore the Royal Blue, Dave Hickson, and he scored the winning goal, despite being covered in blood from a head injury. He played the whole second half holding a sponge to cover the gash over his eye and all this happened after he had fought with the trainer and the ref to stay on the pitch to help the team. I hope you read this, Dunc. Another wonderful one for me was beating Fulham 4-1 (I was in the Paddock for this one) to win the League for the first time since the War. And what about the '66 Cup Final? **Eric (Windsor, Ontario) (05/03/01)**

Can anyone recall this great goal?
Leeds v Everton
1968/69 season
23 November 1968
Everton: West, Wright, Brown, Kendall, Labone, Harvey, Husband, Ball, Royle, Hurst, Morrissey.
THIS GAME WILL ALWAYS stick in my mind at Elland Road against a great Leeds side: Bremner, Giles, Lorrimer etc. My older brother took me with his mates over the Pennines – no M62 then. I was only 13 years old. Everton were on an unbeaten run – Ball, Harvey and Kendall; say no more. The Everton away following was fantastic. The days when following them home and away was affordable to everyone.

   We lost 2-1, but what sticks in my mind was Everton's goal by a certain Joe Royle in front of the travelling away fans, which was on 'Match of the Day' that evening. It was a free kick chipped in delicately from the edge of the penalty area by Alan Ball, that appeared to be harmlessly going to land in Gary Sprakes' hands, about waist high. When a certain Joe Royle dived superbly horizontally to deftly glance the ball off the back of his head over the stunned Leeds keeper's shoulder, into the net. It must have been a training ground exercise executed to perfection. They did not have Goal of the Season then, did they? It will always stick in my mind as the best executed goal I have ever seen. We returned home through the pea soup fog to just get back to watch it on MOTD. **Mark (29/01/01)**

Everton 3 Arsenal 3

5 May 1933

I WAS 11 YEARS OLD when I went to my first Football League
match. I lived in Everton so had to be an Evertonian (still am).
What a period! (1927-1933). League Champions, relegated for
the first time, back in the 1st Division straight away. Cup Winners
1933. Sandwiched between was another Championship, plus
Dixie Dean breaking the long-standing record of 59 goals scored
by Cramsell of Middlesbrough. A hat-trick scored by Dixie to
bring his goal tally in League matches to 60, and a total of 100
in all games played in the season 1927/28.

On a lovely spring day, Saturday, of course, playing Arsenal
with 3 goals wanted, Dixie's name was on everyone's lips.
Arsenal dampened the crowd's cheering (full house, 60,000), by
scoring very early on. Dixie put the score level shortly before
half-time. Dixie was pulled down in the penalty area. Only one
man could take it, and he did, 2-1. Only one more wanted. An
own goal by O'Donnell, 2-2. The result of the game was
incidental. All the Everton players were feeding Dixie, time was
ebbing away. Everton forced a corner. Alec Troup placed the
ball on the spot. The crowd was silent. Next second Goodison
roared. Dixie had headed the third goal. The record was his.
What a man! Arsenal made it 3-3, who cared? We were
Champions again, and the top goal scorer – 60 goals from the
League games 100 goals with Cup and Internationals. One
thing which will never be beaten. **Cyril Taylor aged 84 from
Allerton (28/09/00)**

EXCLUSIVE COLIN HARVEY INTERVIEW

WE MET THE WHITE PELE at a nice little pub in Aughton. We asked him the questions you sent to Blue Kipper, plus a few of our own. Here are Colin's answers.

BK: What was your proudest moment in an Everton shirt?

CH: Every time I put on the Everton shirt was a proud occasion, but if I had to pick, there would be three occasions that stick in the memory. There was my debut at the San Siro. Secondlly, scoring in the semi-final of the 1966 Cup Final against Man United. Thirdly, scoring against West Brom in the game that clinched the Championship for Everton. I didn't get many goals, so it was always a special occasion when I did score! Can you think of anything better than scoring for Everton as an Evertonian?

BK: You have talked about the San Siro debut being a great occasion. When did you know you were playing?

CH: It was on the afternoon of the game. We had lunch and then we had a team meeting. Harry Catterick said there would be only one change. He said, "Denis Stevens – you move to number four and Colin Harvey goes to number eight." This was all because Gabby was injured at the time. It was as simple as that! I just gasped, I didn't have a clue that I was going to play – it was a great way of doing it, he didn't give me a chance to think about it, I just had to go out there and play. I thought no one was going to expect too much of me, I just went out there and did my best and I did okay.

BK: The Italians had a few rough players, one was named Horst Syzmaniak playing for them that day. How did the Italians go about stopping the Everton team?

CH: Yes, I remember him, they could only play three foreigners at that time and he was brought in just to play the European games as a stopper. It was a real tough game, a very, very big step up for me. When you consider that I played for the reserves against Sheffield United on the Saturday and then against the Italians on the Wednesday – it was pretty amazing. The pace was really frantic, but all considering, I really enjoyed it and I played reasonably well. But it was back to the reserves the following Saturday!!

BK: Who, of your peers, did you think was the most exciting player to have played with?

CH: Without question it was Alan Ball. I played against Alan quite often when he was at Blackpool with the C, B and A teams and the reserves. When he finally came to Everton, he was probably the best player in the country, and was probably the best player that ever played for Everton.

BK: During your playing career with Everton who is the best goalkeeper you have played with, or against?

CH: Well, there is no other than Gordon West – he was a bit eccentric, he was certainly off the wall, but what a fantastic goalkeeper he was. As an all-time Everton goalie, there was only Neville who bettered him. He probably won't be happy with me saying that, and he will certainly have a word with me when he sees me next, but Gordon was an exceptional goalie.

BK: I first saw you at White Hart Lane in December 1964. That day you played your first 1st team game at wing-half. Had you played at wing-half before that game?

31

CH: I did actually prefer wing-half; I played in that position at junior levels. A wing-half was a little bit different from an inside forward – it was more of a defensive role. I had to mark Jimmy Greaves that day because that's what Harry Catterick told me to do, but Jimmy still scored! I had a pretty good level of stamina and could get from box to box, but I did prefer the more defensive role. I did seem to get more involved in that position. Joe Royle always reminded me that once I got into the box I got a nose bleed! So I was the one who played that holding role.

BK: Whose idea was it for John Hurst to wear number ten while playing centre-back, with Howard Kendall wearing four and you number six? Was it Harry Catterick's, or one of the players ?

CH: It was my idea to wear the number six; it was always the number I wanted to wear. If you wore the number ten everyone seemed to think that you were the attacking mid-field player. I had to go in and ask Catterick if I could wear the number six and I can tell you, I was shitting myself when I went in! He was great, he said that if that was what I wanted, I could go ahead and wear it. It was a psychological thing really, it just meant that I didn't have the extra responsibility of scoring goals, which as you know, I wasn't very good at! John Hurst was alright about it, so long as he was playing, it didn't bother him. Even Liverpool copied us with Tommy Smith wearing the number ten for some time.

BK: In April 1968, you wore number three away to Sheffield United. Did you actually play left-back at that game?

CH: I never ever played left-back, I really can't remember. It may have been when I'd come back from injury and someone was playing well with the number six, so maybe I just got thrown the number three shirt. I will check it out!

BK: I'm sure I saw you score a goal in about 1968, or '69, at the Street End, against, I think, QPR. You dribbled two defenders, lobbed a third, and then, just inside the box, instead of your usual Row Z, or corner flag finish, you just placed it perfectly in the bottom corner for the most fantastic goal. Do you remember it? Did you ever score a better goal?

CH: I think I remember the goal you're talking about, but I think it was against West Brom. I can't argue against the Row Z thing, because I wasn't a goal scorer, but it was a proud moment and I do remember the goal. It was a good finish, which was unusual for me. I don't know what it was about me and goal scoring, I probably got more and more conscious about it because I didn't score many goals.

BK: Colin, you were the least prolific scorer of the Holy Trinity, but you scored some very important goals for the Blues along the way. Which was your favourite, the semi-final winner against Man U in 1966, or the title clincher v West Brom in 1970? Or do you have a different favourite?

CH: It's probably the semi-final goal, because it was near the end of the game and it was the goal that got us to the final. The other one was a better goal, but it was the second goal, because Alan Whittle had scored the first, and we were always going to beat West Brom anyway. We battered them that night. But the Man United goal was really the one that got us to the Cup Final and that's always something special and that will always be a proud moment of mine.

BK: A game at Goodison saw us beaten by Blackburn 4-2 (Fred Pickering hat-trick). I remember the team, but especially you getting some stick from the crowd. How did you cope with this? Did you ever think football wasn't for you during the early days?

CH: Yes, when I got into the side, I got a fair bit of stick. When you think that at that time I was coming in and sometimes wearing Roy Vernon's shirt, it was difficult replacing him because Roy was one of the Gods! Sometimes I wore number eight shirt in place of Alec Young, so to replace those players was always going to be hard. Obviously, if you didn't play particularly well, you got some stick. It was just a fact of life and you had to get on with it. Harry Catterick was brilliant at that time, he would tell the papers that I'd had a great game, even though I hadn't. It was just his way of sticking up for me. It started to turn for me when I played in the Fairs Cup against Kilmarnock and I managed to get a goal. It seemed to go better and better after that. But getting stick wasn't good when it seemed like sixty thousand people were giving you a hard time, but you just had to stick at it and you come through.

BK: Did you think at that time that because you were a local lad that you got more stick than the others?

CH: Yes, possibly, because at that time Everton were the millionaire club and they were buying the best players available. Quite a few of the local lads came through and became quite successful, such as John Hurst and Tommy Wright, whereas myself, and the likes of Jimmy Husband and Alan Whittle had to come through the ranks. It was all a part of growing up, getting a bit of stick from the crowd shows your character if you come through it.

BK: The White Pele. How did you feel getting this nickname?

CH: It was when I made my debut for Sheffield Wednesday at Bolton. My Dad had brought me back and I got a few phone calls asking how the game had gone, and someone told me that there was a banner at the Park End at Goodison saying something about me and The White Pele – it was a very proud moment for me! For someone to say that about you – comparing you to probably the best player that ever played the game – is really unbelievable. To think that people thought that much of me was hard to believe.

34

BK: It was a major surprise when we sold Alan Ball to the Arsenal. What were your thoughts on hearing the news?

CH: I was Bally's biggest fan – at that time he was probably the best player in Britain. But Bally at that time was not playing his best football, and I certainly don't know why Mr Catterick made the decision to sell him. He obviously had his own reasons, but I don't know them. But it was still a great surprise and Bally went on to prove what a great player he was at Arsenal. I can't say anything against Harry Catterick – in my eyes, he didn't get the credit he deserved. They talk about Shankley, Nicholson and Revie, but he never seems to get a mention, but his record was absolutely fantastic. He didn't spend much time on the training field, it wasn't his style, but in the dressing room and everything else, he was top class. He always seemed to put his finger on what was wrong, and he was spot on.

BK: Who taught you to run so stylishly – with your thumbs stuck out?

CH: I really don't know – when you look at it now, it really looks daft doesn't it? I think it was just the way I ran at the time. I don't like watching videos of myself. I think it was just concentration, I just did it automatically, I don't know why! It's only when you look at a video of yourself and you say "Oh shit! Is that me?" I certainly wasn't aware that I was doing it at the time.

BK: Old kits were not fashionable, as they were all very similar. Where did the tie-ups showing, and just a bit of shirt out the shorts come from?

CH: I suppose I was just copying one of my heroes, actually. Maybe it was Roy Vernon, or Bobby Collins, at the time.

BK: Did you and Bally have a sideburns competition?

CH: No, it was just the style at the time. We all seemed to have big sidees! I didn't shave during pre-season and sometimes we could have six to seven days' growth. It's certainly not like today where they come in with their shaving stuff. The only time we went out was a Saturday night and that was the only time we shaved. The rest of the time we didn't bother. The only thing on our minds at that time was how fit we could get, we didn't think about how our hair looked.

BK: Your one and only England cap must have been a huge honour but also a huge disappointment that you didn't build on it. Why do you think this was? Clearly not through lack of talent.

CH: To be fair, Alf Ramsey at the time was building a club side and he stuck with his players. I got in the squad in 1969 to go to South America before the 1970 World Cup. I was probably playing the best football of my career at that time. I thought I had a really good chance of getting in the World Cup squad, but round about Christmas time I had a serious eye problem and that set me back about three months because the injury prevented me from running, jogging, or any sudden movement at all. I didn't miss many games because there were a lot of call-offs at that time, but I did lose the level of fitness and by the time the end of the season came when we won the Championship, I could have gone on for another couple of months, because I was getting fit again. Because of that, I missed out going to the World Cup.

BK: Who was the player that you were in competition with at that time?

CH: Well, you had the likes of Peter Storey, Alan Mullery, Nobby Stiles and Colin Bell. All top class players and once you were established in Alf's team, it was hard for anybody else to get in.

BK: Also, is it true that Alan Ball used to tell opposing players that their wives were dogs and every time they received the ball he would bark?

CH: No, no – I never heard anything like that! He was the most confident player that I had ever seen. While playing with him, there were times when he would sit on the ball, point to his wrist and ask the crowd what time it was! He was a great believer in his own ability, he was cocky off the field, but he wasn't a big head, he was just a great player, he was a ball of fire.

BK: Do you see any players around today who remind you of yourself and your ability?

CH: Yes, it's a difficult question, but the player I like at the moment is Paul Scholes. I can see a lot of his moves, especially when he hits the ball with the outside of his foot. It was something that I always tried to do. It's great when you're looking one way and are able to kick the ball in the other direction. His goal scoring ability is something special as well, and that's definitely one thing we don't have in common! I just wish I'd had his ability of scoring goals.

BK: In today's market what would the Holy Trinity be worth?

CH: You just can't answer that, but Bally alone would cost the earth! You just can't put a price on it. People didn't realise what a great player he was, the same as Howard. Howard was a great player as well, it would be interesting to know, but you can't go back twenty to thirty years.

BK: What were the reasons behind you leaving for Sheffield Wednesday? At the time did you think that you would ever come back to Everton?

CH: Coming back – never. I didn't think I'd come back in any capacity. I cried when I went out of the gate, I'll be honest with you – I thought it was the end. I thought the next time I'd come back would be to watch a game. Billy Bingham was manager at the time, and I just didn't seem to fit in with his plans. I was having trouble with my hip and the two seasons before I left I was missing training sessions and a few games. I didn't know what it was at the time, and I can see the way Roy Keane walks now, that he's having the same trouble as I had, but the medical side of the game is so advanced now. Because I wasn't training as hard, my form had dipped, and Billy Bingham had just bought Martin Dobson who was a good player and I wasn't getting a game. I don't care what you say, if you're a footballer, all you want to do is play football on a Saturday afternoon. That was the combination of things, and I just made a quick decision to move. The hip caused great difficulty over the next two years at Sheffield Wednesday, I used to train on a Friday, play on a Saturday then rest until the following Friday and Saturday. It became obvious at that time to call it a day from playing.

BK: Who is the most improved player you've coached from day one to him making the first team?

CH: It's difficult to say. You see, I'm a great believer in when a player walks in the place, they're going to be players if they're good enough. I don't think you can coach people to be good players, they've got it from the day they were born – they can blame their mums and dads! But I am a believer in instilling a work ethic and you can develop players and show them the organisation side of the game. It doesn't matter what I do, if a player can play he can play!

BK: We know your views on Wayne Rooney, which of the new crop of young players coming through has impressed you most?

CH: Ozzie (Leon Osman) is certainly a player that's got a chance, he's got great ability but he's been held back the past couple of years with some serious injuries. It was great to see him pushing for a first team place at the end of last season. I hope he makes it, he's a great kid.

BK: Is Wayne that good?

CH: Yes, he is unbelievable, I have seen him since he was about eleven and I put him in the under-nineteens when he was fourteen and he was definitely the best player on the pitch. He is so strong, he can be anything he wants to be.

BK: You have coached so many up and coming players in your time. Are there any players that should have made but didn't, and why?

CH: If they haven't made it, it's down to them. If you come to a football club like Everton, you've got the best chance in the world to make it, and if you've got the ability and you don't make the most of that, it's down to you and nobody else. We can help along the way, but at the end of the day it's up to the individuals to do it for themselves.

BK: It was well known that Gary Lineker didn't train much. Did anybody else during the mid-eighties have problems with your coaching sessions?

CH: No, I don't think so. Gary always seemed to have a little injury that stopped him from training, but to be honest he wasn't the best footballer I'd ever seen. Put him on a pitch and if he got a chance, he normally put it in. His record speaks for itself, not only Everton, but everywhere he went, he was a phenomenal goal scorer.

BK: Howard Kendall pulled off a master-stroke by asking you to be his right-hand man. What did you bring to the team that dominated the mid-eighties? Were you the bad cop and HK the good cop, to get the best out of the players?

CH: (Laughing) No, we didn't work that way, we worked really well as a team. Howard's strength was that he was very shrewd in judging a player I brought to him. I was very passionate when it came to the training side of things, and about video work as well. It was Howard who pulled it all together. It was certainly a great time to be at the Club and for everyone connected with it. The only disappointing time during that period was that we didn't get to go into Europe with that team. It would have been interesting to see how we would have done.

BK: When Howard Kendall left for sunny climates, did you think you were the one to step into the hot seat?

CH: Well, the year before, Howard had had an offer from Barcelona and he thought seriously about it, and he asked me if I fancied going with him. In all honesty, I didn't want to go – it was all hypothetical and nothing ever came from it, but I just didn't fancy going. The following year, he had the offer from Bilbao and because of the European ban, which really upset him, he thought it was the time to go. He did ask if I wanted to go with him, but again, I decided to stay put. I was asked to take over, it wasn't the ideal situation, but to keep the continuity and keep it going, I accepted the job.

BK: As manager, you bought players like Keown and McCall, who had long and successful careers, and a few others, who didn't. Who was the best player you bought? Who would you most like to have brought to Goodison?

CH: Well, I think you've mentioned him, Keown turned out to be a great player. He's made a fantastic career. He was a strange lad in lots of ways, but get him on the field, he would do the business for you. Stuart was a good all-rounder as well. As for Neil McDonald, he certainly had ability, but for some reason he just didn't produce it as well as he should have done on the field. Neil was absolutely brilliant in training, he could use his left or his right foot, but he was as disappointed as anyone that it didn't turn out for him at Everton. Paddy Nevin was another one who had great skill and was something else, but he probably needed stronger players around him. All in all, I didn't get the blend quite right.

BK: Was there anyone you tried to bring in that could have made your era as manager a more successful one?

CH: Probably the most famous one I didn't get, and he would have been great for us, was Mark Hughes. At the time he was at Barcelona but he was on a loan period at Bayern Munich. Anyway, Jim Greenwood and myself went to see Bilbao play on the Sunday and we stayed overnight with Howard (and survived to tell the tale!). On Monday we flew to see the Barcelona officials but unfortunately, Mark was doing really well at Bayern Munich at the time and they were hoping to sell him to them.

BK: If you had your time as manager again, what would you do different from the first time?

CH: That's very difficult to answer, being manager at Everton was probably the most frustrating time of my career. Every other period during my Everton career we had always won things, I've always been involved with winning teams. I wasn't then – even though we finished fourth, eighth and sixth and we got to the final of the FA Cup, the final of the Simod Cup, the semi-final of the Worthington Cup. I really didn't enjoy being manager, I must be honest. I have got to consider that time as a failure due to the simple fact that we didn't win anything.

BK: Do you think certain players let you down when you were manager?

CH: No, certainly not. I'm a believer that your fate is in your own hands. If players don't play as well as they should do, or they don't turn out as you thought they were going to, that's your fault, isn't it? I'm a great believer in that you are responsible for everything that you do yourself, so if we didn't win anything, I was the only one to blame.

BK: Some people believe that your period as manager was a failure, others argue that it wasn't. Everton have had plenty of failures over the last years. Why was Mike Walker such a disaster?

41

CH: I honestly don't know and can't answer anything to do with Mike Walker's period. But I certainly do consider my time as a manager a failure. Don't forget, we came off the back of a great team during the mid-eighties and we lost a couple of really good players. I didn't capitalise on that period, and I didn't turn it round – I just didn't do it – and again, if you don't win anything, you've failed.

BK: We had a good start to the 88/89 season and we thought Tony Cottee was going to be an all-time legend, why did it not work out that way?

CH: His record for the Club was fantastic, he scored over a hundred goals. It always comes down to the fact that while he was with us, we never won anything. If we had won something, he would have stayed. I certainly won't have a go at Tony, because I thought he was a really good player – I must have done, I paid £2 million for him! At the time it was very close whether he was going to sign for Everton, or Arsenal, but it was great when we got him because when you get someone like that, you know you're going to get goals! It certainly wasn't Tony's fault, we just didn't get the right players around him to win anything.

BK: It appeared that you didn't fancy Kevin Sheedy as a player, why?

CH: No, not at all. I thought that Kevin was a really great player, he scored great goals. He provided great crosses with his left foot. I've heard this a few times from people, but at the end of the day, you try not to be mates with the players because you've got a job to do, and you can't afford to get too close to them. But I certainly appreciated everything that he did for the Club.

BK: Did the arrival of Pat Nevin always mean that Tricky Trev would be leaving, even though he was amongst the best we had at the time?

42

CH: No, not necessarily. I just thought it was a great opportunity to get Pat when he became available. Don't forget, Trevor could play on the left, the middle and even on occasions could play upfront. It certainly wasn't the case of wanting to get rid of Trevor because he was a fantastic player and one of the top twenty Everton players of all time – he really was that good. But once again, because of the European ban, he decided to go to Rangers to play in Europe.

BK: You seemed happier to be a number two, rather than the main man. Any reasons for this?

CH: No, the only reason I wasn't happy was because we didn't win anything.

BK: After giving Graeme Sharp a hard time in training sessions during his early days, what was it like to be his number two?

CH: I never gave him a hard time as such, for me he was such a good player. I was very passionate about the training. The training sessions were hard. Once they were over, things were forgotten about. He was great at Oldham, I have always liked Graeme and we got on really well. I liked him from the day he walked in the place as a kid at Everton. I never had any problems with him, he was great to work for. I had a lot of time for him as a player, and I suppose sometimes you're harder on the ones you like!

BK: What was the best game you were involved in?

CH: The one that sticks out is the 4-0 win at Anfield against Liverpool. I scored in that game and you couldn't have got a better feeling. We had a few reserves out that day, but we really battered them and to score was just brilliant! The rivalry was fiercer then than it is now, especially when they had Tommy Smith and Ron Yeats in their team. It's great to beat them at any time, but that day we weren't expected to win at all, so that game must rank very highly in my memories.

BK: In the past, we've had two great managers – Catterick and Kendall and now we might have a third. You have worked with all of them – how do you rate them?

CH: Well we've spoken about Catterick before and he definitely didn't get the credit he deserved. He was there for about twelve years, he built three or four teams and went on to win championships and cups – he was a great manager. He was a little bit different, he wasn't a tracksuit man at all, but he knew the game inside out. He always knew what the problem was and sorted us out at half-time. You already know my feelings about Howard, he pulled things together and really was special. As for David Moyes, his achievements over the last year have been fantastic. He is very enthusiastic and very thorough, he's done a great job so far. I just hope he can carry it on – he needs to be judged over a longer period of time. I just hope he gets some money to add players to the squad he's got now.

BK: With the announcement of your retirement – is this going to be a complete severing of ties?

CH: Maybe, you just never know. I've had three hip operations, the first one I had done over twenty years ago and I have never had a problem with it since. The other one was done fifteen years ago and was never quite right, I had it re-done about two years ago. It's good enough for me to walk and drive, but not for what I want to do with my coaching. Over the last couple of years it's been getting more and more frustrating and I haven't been able to do my job as well as I should do. So it was the right time to call it a day on the coaching side.

BK: Do you think you have a role to play at Everton in the future?

CH: I don't honestly know, I'm just going to leave it for a while and see how it settles down, and obviously just take it from there.

BK: Your testimonial game against Palma is coming up on Sunday 10 August, I suppose that is going to be something special for you?

CH: Yes, I'm really looking forward to it. It's a pre-season friendly with half the proceeds going to Blueblood, the former Everton Players' Foundation, which is a brilliant idea. I know recently Tommy Wright has just had a knee operation and I know of loads of others who have had great benefits from this charity. It was just a great honour to be asked and a great chance to see everybody again. It's a chance to get to Goodison again as I never said my proper goodbyes when I left.

BK: How would you most like to be thought of and remembered by Evertonians?

CH: To have played for Everton and being an Evertonian myself; and all my family being Evertonians, it would be nice for them to remember me as a good player.

Well Colin, you were more than just a good player, you were one of the all-time greats at Everton – never to be forgotten. You are truly an Everton living legend (02/07/03)

OLD SCHOOL

CLASSIC SHOUTS from days gone by ...

CAN'T RECALL WHICH YEAR it was, only that Colin Harvey was manager and I think we were playing Derby County. I was sat in the Bullens Road with me arl fella, the place was half full and you could hear a pin drop. Next minute me arl fella stood up and shouted, "HEY, KEEP THE FRIGGIN' NOISE DOWN IN THAT CHURCH, WE'RE TRYIN' TO PLAY FOOTBALL IN HERE!" The whole section fell about laughing. **Ravo Junior (09/05/03)**

WHEN I WAS A JUNIOR BLUE I would sit laughing at some of the comments heard coming from the stands! I don't recall the game but, one Saturday, Andrei Kanchelskis was having a blinder! He's taking the ball down the wing with it sticking to his feet like glue and making a mug of the fullback. We were all in awe, when some funny bastard sat next to me in Lower Gwladys Street stands up and shouts, "Eh! Andrei! Are you wearin' suzzies or summat? 'Cos ya turnin' me on!" Never have truer words been spoken! **Yozza (28/04/03)**

PETER SHILTON was in goal for Southampton after being in the paper for a domestic with his missus. Some wag in the Street End shouts, "Eh! Shilton! Yer bastard. It's a pity yer didn't hit Maradonna as hard as yer hit yer missus." Shilton never turned round but raised a hand in acknowledgement – fair play. **Big Dave (28/04/03)**

BACK IN THE LATE 70S, Ipswich Town were at Goodison giving Everton a sound thrashing. Paul Mariner is shouting various tactics to his team mates as Ipswich prepare to take a corner. This bloke in front of us shouts, "Hey! Mariner! There's women and children trying to sleep here." **Thom Lester (01/03/03)**

IT WAS THE FIRST MATCH of the season back in the dark 70s. A Blue in the Gwladys Street saw his mate coming up the terrace and said to him, "You said at the last game of last season that you wouldn't be coming again." His mate said, "It would take more than this fucking lot to keep me away!" **David Evans (04/01/04)**

BACK WHEN PERRY GROVES (reddest of redheads) used to play for Arsenal, he was warming up with his back to us on the touchline in front of the then 'Panini Family Section' (not known for its outbursts). Some fella just stands up in front of us and starts shouting, "Groves! Groves! Hey! Groves!" Eventually – and with a smile on his face – knowing he's gonna get abuse, Perry Groves turns round and faces the fella, who shouts, "Groves! You've got a head like my bell end!" Perry Groves, other Arsenal players warming up, the Everton fans and even the police in earshot all fell about. A classic. **Dave L (13/12/03)**

BACK IN THE 80s, Paul Power's taking a throw-in for City by the Paddock, someone shouts, "Power, you're too old. You've always been too old." Next season we buy him, and what a buy. **Steve White (16/02/02)**

UNDER THE CLOCK, Goodison Road, late 1960s. Brian Labone v Man City. Labby clatters Mike Summerbee face down to the ground. City trainer on for ages. "'Urry up," goes the shout. Fella behind – "Can't. It'll take fuckin' ages to get his nose out the pitch!" **Graham Taylor – the other one! (20/02/02)**

JUST FINISHED THE 'GREAVSIE' BIOG – in it he says there is no decent banter anymore from the crowd – he gives the following as an example from his playing days – 1968/69 season. 'I was in the Everton penalty area, at the Gwladys Street End, waiting for Jimmy Robertson to take a corner, when I heard someone shout, "Greaves, you're over the hill." When Jimmy's corner came across, Alan Gilzean nodded the ball back to me and I volleyed it into the net. Goodison Park fell silent. "Okay, so you're not over the hill," boomed the same Gwladys Street voice, "but you've got a bloody good view of the valley!" **David Harron (13/12/03)**

A FEW YEARS BACK at Goodison, can't remember against who, but the Blues had about six corners at the Park End, each time taken from a different side from the one before by Andy Hinchcliffe. Andy looked knackered running from one side of the park to the other. So someone shouted, "will someone buy 'im a bike for fuck's sake!" Priceless. **Steven Barton (06/04/02)**

AT A HOME GAME around Christmas time in the 70s during a particularly poor match (nothing new then), someone shouts out, "Come on, Everton, it's just like a pantomime." Another wag responds with, "Oh! No it's not!" To which twenty others replied with, "Oh! Yes it is!" Well it amused me anyway. **Bob Thomason (04/02/02)**

MANY MOONS AGO, think it was 1967. We were playing the Albion in a League game, which we won 5-4. John Osborne, the WBA goalie, was, well the politest way to say it, I guess, is that he was visually challenged in the handsome department. Well, after he'd kept the Blue boys at bay one time some even uglier bloke with a leather jacket on in the Street, bellowed at him, "Hey! Osborne! You've got a face like a pan of fried arseholes." To which the ever jovial Osborne dropped his kecks and, let there be no doubt, there was an uncanny similarity twixt face and arse! **Glenn King (19/01/02)**

PLAYING SPURS the season after Mike Walker's departure. Ian Walker is in the nets at the Street End. He's just placed the ball on the 6-yard box, walked to his post to start his run-up to punt the ball forward, when in a moment of almost complete silence, a guy gets up and shouts, "Hey Walker! Yer dad's a wanker and yer crisps are shite!" **Watto the Blue (13/12/03)**

BACK IN ABOUT 1978, we were playing a mid-week Cup game, I think it was Southampton. Strangely enough there were huge queues outside and the kick off was delayed. The police were trying to sort everyone out and someone shouted, "Hey! mate! Let this fella through – he's on crutches." Then a voice from the back shouts, "Aargh, ya lousy bastard, they're mine them!" Priceless. **Neil Quinn (05/12/03)**

A FEW YEARS AGO in the Gwladys, can't remember who we were playing, but Earl Barrett was playing (his usual shite self). He's taking his time with a throw-in and I shout, "Come on, Earl. Hurry up for fuck's sake." Some fella turns round and says, "Is that his name? Earl? I always thought it was Fuck Off!" Pissed meself. **Chrism8 (13/10/03)**

STREET END IN THE 70s, can't remember who we were playing. Someone tries to get a chant going but there's no response. "Whad'ya want ... a solo?" he shouts. "So low we can't fuckin' 'ear yer," came the reply. Brilliant. **Haynes (04/09/02)**

THE GOLDEN VISION playing his usual sublime game. "Christ! he's just great! If I came home and found him in bed with my wife I'd tuck him in!" **Tandy (09/07/02)**

AT A GAME IN THE HALCYON DAYS of the mid-80s. Reidy has the ball, Trev is making a break-out on the right, a voice with instructions for Reidy, "Wing! Wing! Wing!" Another voice, "Will someone answer that fuckin' phone?" Worth the entrance fee. **Blueheart (31/07/02)**

STORY TOLD TO ME by mate Brian. His mate was having a piss and Alex Golden Vision took up the next urinal. "Just splash a few drops on me shoes over here, Alex," was the alleged comment! **Tandy (02/07/02)**

BACK IN 1973/74 we had just been beaten at home by Leeds and me Dad (known to many as Tommy Everton) shouted at the top of his voice, "I'm not coming down until Billy Bingham gets sacked." That may not sound funny, but he was at the top of the floodlights between The Park End and Bullens when he shouted it. I'm not joking, it was on the front page of The Echo. **Brian (12/06/02)**

I REMEMBER TALKING to a Clayhead some years ago, and he had been to see Everton play circa 1969, when Rolf was top of the charts with 'Two Little Boys'. It was the days when the bizzies were able to bring the horses inside Goodison. Anyway, something happened and a bizzy got injured, one of his colleagues on horseback rode across to him to take him to get some help, at which point the Street End broke in as one with, "Did you think I would leave you dyin', when there's room on my horse for two …". **Steve Enty (31/05/02)**

MANY SEASONS AGO, Man City, the visitors. A hopeful boot up the pitch out of defence by one of their defenders. Mike Summerbee, City's wizard-of-the-dribble, blessed with the biggest nasal protuberance ever to grace Goodison, collects the ball and hares off towards the Gwladys Street goal. Up goes the linesman's flag. Summerbee goes ape, waves arms around, stamps feet, yells at linesman, boots ball away. Shout from crowd, "Yer nose was offside, Summerbee!" All around wet themselves (including Summerbee and the linesman). **Blue Peter (07/01/02)**

MANY, MANY YEARS AGO, I was stuck in London over Easter and decided to go to watch West Ham v Ipswich, who had Kevin Beattie playing at centre-half. After 30 minutes Beattie has scored two own goals, a proper one for Ipswich and been booked. Then from an Ipswich corner, he pops up and equalises, causing a stunned silence. Except for the bloke behind me who says, "Get into the fucking game, Beattie!" **Craig Harry (15/10/01)**

IN THE EARLY 80s, Gwladys Street End, there was an old dear, about 4 foot tall, Irish-sounding accent, scarf that looked like a souvenir from the 1933 Cup Final. At one game some young scally sat on a barrier shouted at an opposing striker, "Fuck off you, you're worse than fuckin' Rush!" Old dear pushes through the crowd towards him, furious, and pulls him round by the shoulder. Kid looks terrified. Prodding him in the chest she screams in his ear, "Hey, lad, watch your mouth. There's no need for language like that from a kid like you. There's women and kids round 'ere y'know and they don't want to hear stuff like that. I hear you mention that fuckin' ugly big-nosed bastard's fuckin' name again, I'll fuckin' slap yer!" Cue applause. **John Williams (29/09/01)**

EXCLUSIVE DEREK MOUNTFIELD INTERVIEW

WE MET DEGGSEY IN A QUIET LITTLE ESTABLISHMENT at the Albert Dock before the end of the season.

BK: As a big Evertonian playing for Tranmere, how did you feel when you found out that Everton were interested in your signature?

DM: I'll say this to anybody, there is no better feeling than being asked to play for the team you have watched from the terraces. I was still watching Everton when I was playing for Tranmere, if there was no game, I'd be on the terraces. When I first joined Tranmere in '79 I still had a season ticket, so if I wasn't involved in a game I'd be at Goodison. One Thursday afternoon, we were training in the far corner of Tranmere's ground before going to Blackpool for our end of season jaunt, Brian Hamilton called out, "Over yer come, Derek" and I thought, "What have I done?" Brian said, "We've talked about you and have agreed a deal but they want to have a look at you first." It's Howard Kendall and Everton! What do you do? Youíre speaking to Howard Kendall, someone you watched as a kid. Just to sign for the Club was a dream come true. No matter who I played for, I was always an Evertonian, always have been, always will be – simple as that.

BK: You came as a virtual unknown player …

DM: … and left as an unknown player!

BK: and became established in a great team. Who was it in the squad who helped you settle in?

DM: It's hard to say, I became good friends with Gary Stevens – and still am to this day – as we lived fairly close to each other and used to take it in turns to drive into training. But for me the biggest influence on my first year at Everton was Colin Harvey – he was looking after the reserves at the time and there was myself, Gary, Kevin Richardson, and we'd just brought in Alan Harper and Kevin Sheedy. We had the experienced players Howard had brought in – the likes of Alan Biley, Alan Ainscow and Mick Ferguson and Colin used to make sure those players trained with us at least twice a week. Colin Harvey worked so hard on me and the other young players, you ask any players of that era and they have always got a lot to say about Colin Harvey as a coach, he helped me enormously and gave me an understanding of what I needed to work on. I never have been a complete player, but Colin made me a better player and is one of the best coaches I've ever worked with.

BK: Presumably it was Reidy and Andy Gray who were the dressing room motivators – is this right?

DM: They came in with tremendous enthusiasm and will to win. I think if someone's got that will to win it's bound to rub off on the people around them. They had a big part to play, but also John Bailey was a great character in the changing rooms. He couldn't go anywhere without taking the piss out of someone, or something. Anyone who was around the Club in those days knows what it was like. Two years before that I was playing at the bottom of the then Fourth Division, in front of crowds of around a thousand, then all of a sudden I'm playing in front of fifty thousand against Bayern Munich. Yes, those two individuals had a great influence on what happened but we had great nucleus and I think it just clicked at the right time.

BK: What dressing room motivational moments do you particularly remember?

DM: The one that everyone talks about was the Bayern Munich game, we'd come in at half-time 1-0 down and Howard basically said, "You've won it! Get out there and play the same way." The biggest thing about that night was the whole build-up to the game – the atmosphere outside and inside the ground – and then when we came out for the second half I can honestly say it's the one and only time I shat myself because the roar was incredible. But after Howard saying, "You've won it!" we went out with so much confidence. Other than that I can't remember anything specific being said before a game, or at half-time, because once we got on a roll, if we went 1-0 down after thirty seconds, like against Sunderland, we always knew we'd come back and win the game, as we had so much self belief and self-confidence.

BK: I have always wondered what the atmosphere at Goodison was like during the glory days of the eighties. Was it different from Goodison nowadays?

DM: It's difficult to say, because if you look at the average attendance it's probably higher now than what is was in the mid-eighties but football has changed so much in those fifteen or so years. The Bayern Munich game was exceptional and I've never played in a game like it. We used to go to the St George's Hotel (Holiday Inn now) every mid-week home game. We'd have a meal at Goodison at lunchtime, then go down there for the afternoon, allegedly lying in bed relaxing, although some didn't. I remember getting back on the coach about six o'clock and we couldn't get the coach down the Street End because of the number of people. It was like Moses parting the waves, there was just this sea of blue and one by one they'd move aside to let the coach through. It was phenomenal. It's different now because it's a different type of game, more family-orientated and what you haven't got now is terraces. I'd love to stand on the terraces in the Street End again, but you can't because of the all-seater stadium and I

56

think that has changed the atmosphere entirely. There is not as much singing and chanting as there was in the eighties. I do want to go in the Street End again as a fan but I want to stand there, not sit there.

BK: Do you think that will ever happen?

DM: I hope so, for me the game is crying out for some terracing to bring some of the atmosphere back to the grounds. The all-seater stadiums have given us much better conditions, but I do think we have lost some of the atmosphere since the terraces have gone.

BK: Going back to Peter Reid and Andy Gray – who in your opinion was the more aggressive?

DM: Pat van den Hauwe.

BK: Funnily enough, Sheeds said he would back the Rat against Psycho in a fifty/fitfy.

DM: Well, they were both aggressive players, who would do everything within the boundaries of the game to win. But there were some players who were nasty as well. As for Andy Gray he was just a born leader, on the pitch he was a different class and an integral part of our success. Peter was a different type of player – snappy, aggressive, a get-it-and-give player who blossomed at Everton. He was a has-been and crock two years earlier who became one of the best players in the world for those two or three years.

BK: What would you say was the biggest single reason for our success in the 1980s?

DM: You tell me. People say it was the Oxford game that turned us around, others say it was Colin Harvey coming up from the reserves, we just seemed to click at the right time. I remember playing those two dreadful games over Christmas '83. Coventry at home on Boxing Day, 0-0, and we were poor, then the next day we went down to Wolves and got beaten 3-0. I remember speaking to Wayne Clark when he came to

57

Everton and he said we were the worst team they had played that season. After that we played Birmingham away round about New Year. We had that silver away kit and the referee said it would clash with their kit under the floodlights, so we had to wear their yellow and blue away kit. We won 2-0 and then went on a good run. I believe Colin Harvey had a lot to do with it and just clicking at the right time. But there is no single reason. There's a bit of luck in there. Yes, Andy Gray had a lot to do with it, as did us getting a settled side. We'd had quite a few changes early on that season but after Christmas we had a settled back four and once you get the nucleus of a team with eleven players playing regularly, you get an understanding. So all these things combined to put us in a situation that we'll talk about for years to come.

BK: How did you get the black eye you had in the Luton semi-final?

DM: Mick Hartford. He bust my nose and splattered my eye that day and he's probably the nastiest centre forward I played against. He was an honest, hard, committed player but wasn't afraid to use his elbows. I can't remember the actual incident, but I remember my eye was rather big and shut by the Sunday morning.

BK: Is it unusual to get a black eye during the game.

DM: No, it happened a lot, as I didn't used to cut, so I'd bruise instead.

BK: What was your funniest memory of that time?

DM: Not really sure, as there were so many. It probably involved Bails, or perhaps when Ratts scored from thirty-five yards and then giving Bruce a tenner for doing it (All said in jest – lawyers need not respond). But you have so many laughs when you're in the game, it's hard to pick out and remember one. The happiest time was the FA Cup Final win because we had a fantastic time the same night.

BK: What was your proudest moment?

DM: Again, at that time there were so many things to be proud of.
        Was it winning the League, the Cup, the Cup Winners Cup?
        I'm not sure, certainly one of the proudest was going round
        town on the Sunday after winning the FA Cup on the open top
        bus. My Mum and Dad had told me where they were going to
        be and I had the Cup in my hands when we went past them.
        And just to see the Everton fans out in such force was fantastic.
        Once you've done one of those bus tours you just want to do it
        again, because you see the pride in people's faces. You don't
        know what to expect but to actually parade the Cup feels like
        you have done something special. That really was a proud
        day.

BK: A bobby's motorbike on the '84 homecoming bus route on
        Scotty Road hit a fan. The fan was shouting your name, and
        you waved just as the bike hit him. He remembers you waved
        the same way as you celebrated scoring with your fingers
        splayed out wide. How do you feel about being responsible for
        his near death?

DM: I don't remember anyone getting hit by a police motorbike, but
        thank god it was only a near death and not an actual death
        and he's still alive to support the Club. As I've said, it was
        such a great day, with so many things happening, but I don't
        think it was my fault (panicking) and he should have stayed
        behind the police cordon anyway (laughing).

BK: Who was the best player you have played against?

DM: Probably got to be Michel Platini. We played in a testimonial
        game over at Leeds for John Charles and Bobby Collins and
        he played in midfield. What an array of skills and passing he
        had. It was only a slow-paced game, but he was phenomenal.
        When I'm asked who was the best centre forward I played
        against I put it down to three categories. The best pairing –
        that had to be those two from across the park. The hardest

man to get the ball off has got to be Mark Hughes, he had a body which seemed to be about six feet wide, getting round his arse was like going on a two-mile detour. And the nastiest was Mick Harford (see question above). I was fortunate to play against all different types of players. You've got the likes of Gazza and Brian Robson, the likes of Terry Butcher, who played with his heart, then Glenn Hoddle who had magnificent skills. For strikers I'd say those three, but number one was Michel Platini. When you see him close up, and he's picking players out from forty yards, he really was phenomenal. That was when he was coming to the end of his career. He must have been an awesome player. He impressed me so much. I never got his shirt either!

BK: Who did you kick the most?

DM: I didn't go out to kick anyone intentionally, but I had a few spats and fights with Mick Harford and Mark Hughes. The thing was you'd kick them, and you knew they would kick you back. You didn't go down moaning (Derek makes the sound of a dying cat) rolling over, doing a triple salchow. You got up and kicked them back again. In the 1986 FA Cup Final, I went right into Dalglish, right up his backside. Ten minutes later he I went for a header, and he put his studs right down my thigh. You played hard, but I never went out to kick someone.

BK: Do you think that if we'd kept the young team of the mid-eighties, we would have been as successful and as dominant in the late eighties?

DM: Well, that's the sixty-four million dollar question. I have actually got to do a piece in a book called 'What If'. For example, what if we hadn't had the unfortunate incident at Heysel – what would we have done? One of my biggest regrets in football is winning the Football League twice and never getting the chance to compete in Europe – what could we have done in Europe in the 1985/86 season? We don't know, we'll never know. If this incident hadn't happened, I'm sure we would have kept the squad together, and who knows what we could have achieved. But that's just an opinion – we'll never know. It would have been great to have looked back and instead of having two or three years' success, maybe having six or seven. It will always be the greatest talking point of the mid-eighties.

BK: What was your initial reaction when the Club signed Dave Watson and the start of the 86/87 season?

DM: If you look back at that time, we had a spate of injuries like Gary Stevens and Pat van Den Hauwe. Howard could have signed a right-back, a left-back, he could have signed anybody – he decided to sign Dave Watson. I hoped at the time that he wasn't there to replace me, but when you pay nearly a million pounds for someone, you know he's going to go straight into the team. Nowadays, you can pay a lot of money for somebody, and they are just a squad player. In the eighties we only had a small squad. I knew it was going to be a scrap and a battle to keep my place, but unfortunately for me, Howard stuck with Dave. He was a wonderful player for the Club, he played over five hundred games and had success. Unfortunately for me, that was the nail in my coffin which forced me to leave the Club and further my career. I have nothing but respect for Dave and don't hold any grudges whatsoever. You could say he was a phenomenal player and captain for the Club.

BK: Do you look back at Everton at that time with a tinge of regret, or do you look back at the good times?

DM: Oh, I certainly look back at the good times. Those good times are in the record books and I have got the trophies to go with them and I've always got the pictures and the memories. If I look back and ask myself whether I should I have given it a bit longer I just think, well, Dave came in the summer of '86 and I spent two years trying to break back into the side. It didn't matter how well I played, I was always hauled back in the reserves. I was playing in the reserves and then I was always either sub, or the thirteenth man the following week. I was going around the country as the then thirteenth man. No matter how well I played, I just couldn't get back into the side. When Howard left and Colin took over, the same happened again, so I decided I had to get away to get my football going again. Maybe if I had stayed for the third year, I might have broken back into the side. It was difficult after playing for two full seasons, the next two seasons I managed less than twenty-eight games. When you've had the highs, been to Wembley, played in FA Cups, been in Europe in Cup Finals and winning the League Championships, I wasn't playing football! So I left really to get my football going again. Looking back, it was probably the wrong thing to do, maybe I should have stuck it out for a bit longer. I had the chance to play first team football in the 1st Division, and I had to take the chance.

BK: When Dave Watson came in, we lost your contribution in goals – what are your views on this?

DM: Well I scored twenty-six goals in two years, you don't expect that from a centre half, but Dave was a different player from me. Dave was aggressive and wholehearted. But as I've said before, when someone pays one million pounds for a player … Howard gave Dave enough time to settle in and you can't take anything away from Dave with him playing five hundred games. Basically, Dave was the reason I had to leave the Club. I wasn't the only one that was in this position. Kevin Richardson left the Club because he couldn't get a game and John Bailey left the Club because of being replaced by Pat Van Den Hauwe, Andy Gray had to leave because they brought Lineker in – but they'll never be able to take away the memories that I've got playing over one hundred and fifty games for the Club.

BK: Your goal tally in 84/85 proved that you had an excellent eye for an opportunity, especially from set pieces. You not only headed goals but other great strikes as well. Did you ever play as a striker in your earlier days?

DM: Yeah, I played in my earlier days as a centre forward most of the time and scored plenty of goals and won plenty of trophies, once scoring a hat-trick in a Cup Final. When I first went to Tranmere as a schoolboy I went there as a centre forward, but was soon put back as a centre half. Really, talking about the goals I scored, – when you've got Kevin Sheedy and Trevor Steven putting quality balls into the box, you can't help scoring goals! There was no special knack or art to scoring, but when you get quality service like those two lads were putting in, any centre half would score! When I went to Villa, I got it again with Gordon Cowans – he was another one that could provide quality service. I think I got something like nineteen goals, most of them from Gordon's quality crosses.

BK: I think you are doing yourself a bit of disservice there.

DM: Ah! Well, there was a bit of luck involved, a bit of movement – I knew where the goal was, but if I had taken every chance, I would have won the gold boot every year!! The thing was, Ratty never went up for set players, and I was always the one, so I probably had my fair share of chances. When one came along, I just tried to put it in the back of the net. I scored some great goals, and I scored some flukey goals, there is always a bit of luck involved.

BK: Do you remember the goal you scored in the 1-1 draw at Old Trafford? What can you tell us about that?

DM: I remember that Olsen scored for them from an off-side position. I remember in the second half, Trevor Steven got a corner in the Stretford End. As he was taking it, he got hit by a coin. He put it in, Terry Curran got a flick on and I arrived about fifteen foot in the air and headed it so hard down that it should have hit the floor and then gone over the crossbar, but fortunately, it bounced in the top of the net. Yeah, a lot of people always remind me about that one!

BK: Another everyone talks about, Derek, is the goal you scored and your celebration in the semi-final at Villa Park. What are your memories?

DM: Well, everyone's got their own celebrations. If you look at the different celebrations over the years, you will remember Mick Channon's windmill. People run away with one finger in the air like Alan Shearer, I used to run away like a headless chicken! For me, it was just a bonus to score for Everton – I'd just scored a goal for the team I supported. But I've actually got a picture of that one when Andy Gray is strangling me around the neck, pointing to the dugout saying that we're back in it now. It's a great black and white picture that I've got framed on my wall.

BK: Okay, Derek, now for the funny bits. The muzzy – why? With a moustache like yours, did anyone approach you to star in a porno movie? Do you think they'll make a come-back in football?

DM: I don't know why I had it! I had it for many years and when I actually took it off, people didn't realise that I'd had a moustache in the first place! I took it off one night, put it on the side of the couch and it stood up and crawled away! No – I've never been asked to do a porn movie, and no, I can't see moustaches making a come-back, I think they are, thankfully, a thing of the past! Funny thing is, people never mention Gary Steven's moustache in the 1984 Cup Final. He refused to shave until we got beat in the Cup, so check it up by looking at all your old videos! But I don't miss it, it's been gone for over ten years.

BK: What defender inspired you in the playground and what qualities did you try and emulate?

DM: If I am honest, as an Everton fan, I was a big fan of Bob Latchford 'cos I was a centre forward when I was a kid. But

Mick Lyons takes some beating as a true Evertonian, As a kid, I watched centre forwards, 'cos I loved banging the goals in, so I never focused on the centre halves at all. I used to watch the goal scorers. The only centre halves from the mid 70s/mid 80s were the likes of Mick Lyons and Roger Kenyon, 'cos I used to watch them. I used to have this big thing about Martin Dobson who was a hell of a player but Latch was the goal scorer and he was the one I used to love watching.

BK: I know we've touched on this before, but who was your best friend at Everton?

DM: I still see Gary now and speak to him on a regular basis. I wasn't a great socialiser and didn't go out for a drink all the time, but we used to live close and we used to take turns going to training in the car. I always say hello and have a chat to the lads and I still see Bails on a regular basis, but Gary was probably the closest one in the Club at that time.

BK: Who in the modern game would you consider to be the most similar to yourself in their style of play? Tricky one!

DM: I don't know, I think in football now, centre halves have become better footballers. In my day, the centre half was there to defend and I think that's where a lot of defenders now fall down. First and foremost you're a defender and secondly, then you're a footballer. You see a lot of players now trying to play football when they can't and they shouldn't. So my job was to clear the ball and if it meant putting the ball in Row Z, or Stanley Park, I'd do it. It gives everyone the chance to reboot and get back together. If there's one centre half you've got to take your hat off to over the last ten to fifteen years you've got to look at Tony Adams. I think he's been outstanding. If it hadn't of been for Arsene Wenger I think he'd have finished football three or four years earlier.

BK: What did you think of your time managing Cork City and what did you think of the League in Ireland?

DM: Cork City was a learning curve for me. I got the job and went in there with all the best intentions of doing it right. Unfortunately, it didn't work out, and there were things that I would have liked more support over and there were things I did wrong, but everyone in life makes decisions and you learn from your mistakes. The League of Ireland is a very, very competitive league and there are quite a lot of very good players who have come over here. Roy Keane and Dennis Irwin, who come from Cork, have made good careers out of the game. But Irish football has to make that next step and become more professional as a league and as individual clubs. If there's one problem with Cork it's that it's so isolated down south – any trip to Dublin takes four to five hours, so I didn't have the chance to watch enough games while I was there, which I regret. I did things wrong, I did things right, I tried to make them more professional and tried to introduce things to them, but it was a learning curve for me. I tried to do my best, but sometimes my best wasn't good enough.

BK: Do you think we should stay and redevelop Goodison, or move elsewhere?

DM: This is the big debate. This was first mentioned seven or eight years ago when Peter Johnson was governor and we all shouted him down for being a Red Nose. We don't want to move, yet Bill Kenwright brought the idea back up two or three years ago and we all said, "Great idea, Bill". If you look at Goodison Park now compared to many of the premiership stadiums, we're very much outdated. We all agree that we've got obstructed views, old stands. We need to do something, whether we redevelop Goodison, or we move away from the place, we don't know. I work down at the Albert Dock and I park the car in ninety-nine mile per hour winds – I can't imagine what that would have done to a football ground with a game on. I didn't think Kings Dock was the right venue, purely because of the logistics of getting in and out. If we

66

move, we've got to move for the right reasons. To maintain that we've got to concentrate on everybody; the fans, ask them what they want, the players etc. It's got to be right, we don't just want to go and build a stand or stadium that isn't really fan-friendly. If we do move I'll be there to collect a piece of Goodison Park to put in my house, whether it be my old peg where I used to sit, or part of the changing room, or part of the pitch. I will want something to remember my times at Goodison, not only as a player, but also as a fan. If we do move, we're going to move, to hopefully, a super stadium which will better Everton in the future.

BK: What's your opinion of the state of football for disabled young kids?

DM: I really don't know much about football for the disabled. I know we have a disabled football team in the Club. If you look at disability, you're looking at racism as well. We have got to make football more and more user friendly, we've got to make things right for the kids – they are the future of the Club. We have got to make the facilities better for everybody. I work with disabled people and they are as committed to football and sport as anybody is and maybe we have to look again at whatever we can do to help them.

BK: When you scored and when Sharpy scored, you never seemed to congratulate each other, whereas everyone else mobbed each other, was there anything in that?

DM: No, nothing. He called me a boney bastard! Whenever I scored, Andy Gray was always the first one there. Nowadays, there are big celebrations and all that stuff. We used to jump on each other, but no, there was nothing in it, unless Sharpy has said something else!

NO ONE IS SAFE

YER PAYS YER MONEY, yer have the right to make yerself heard. Even our own (some not so) beloved boys in Blue can't escape from the wrath of fans.

AT THE RECENT SPURS GAME, Rodrigo was warming up when Rhino ran passed him on the touch line, also warming up. A shout from the Main Stand, "I bet Rivaldo's shittin' himself with pace like that, lad." Welcome to Goodison, Rodders. **Gary Gallagher (23/08/02)**

WAS AT RHINO'S TESTIMONIAL, when Bilbao's keeper went down injured like all the rest of the team. Fucking tarts. Anyway, he's lying there on the floor and somebody behind shouts, "Give them, Gerrard." We all thought it was a great idea. **Dave (19/08/02)**

LEICESTER v EVERTON. Brian Dean scores and everyone's booing him, some fella shouts, "Come on, Gerrard. Keep yer head up, lad." Then some fella shouts, "Why? He'll most probably drop that as well." **Gary Jones (31/07/02)**

WHILE WATCHING last season's 2nd round League Cup defeat to Crystal Palace. Tal (playing his usual shite) got a knock and went on the floor. As the physio legged it on to the pitch me arl fella shouts, "You useless bastards, why can't you all run like him!" **EFCLad (21/06/02)**

IT WAS ABOUT 1997, in the Joe Royle era, at a night match, Earl Barrett was playing to his usual shite best. The ball got played across the back-line and ended up at good old Earl on the right. At this point some fella shouts, "Don't pass to Barrett, he can't control his piss, never mind the ball." It still makes me laugh now! **Graeme Stanley (03/06/02)**

WE WERE IN THE MAIN STAND at the boring Southampton game, just before David Weir's attempted 20-yard drive, when an old bloke shouted, "Hit the fucking thing!" Almost immediately the ball came gunning towards us, to which this bloke replied, "Not at us, you stupid Scotch twat!" Best cheer of the whole game. **Gary Sutton (17/11/03)**

ON A TYPICAL cold, miserable Saturday afternoon during what are now regarded as 'the Smith years', I was in the Paddock, along with a group of others. My attention was drawn to a plastic bag which had blown up and down the Bullens Road touch line several times. As the linesman bent to pick it up some wag shouted, "Leave it there, it's doing more than fucking Alexandersson." Absolutely spot on. **Blue Jim (13/10/03)**

ME AND ME MATE were at the Everton v Leicester game last season and, as per usual, Gerrard was having a shite game. Gerrard and Stubbs fucked up and let the first goal in for Leicester and we were gutted. The highlight of the match for us was when Everton got a free-kick in our area and someone passed the ball back to Gerrard so he could take it. He caught the ball and some geezer next to us shouted, "Well held." Ha Ha, we were in stitches. **Bez and Smithy (16/07/02)**

AT THE BOLTON GAME, the Rad's just missed his third easy chance, and the fella behind me goes, "You know, I reckon Thomasz Radzinski is the best player ever to play for Everton Football Club ..." We all sat waiting for the punch line, then it came, "... with two 'z's in his name." Main Stand was pissin' itself. Cheers. **Chris Butland (29/04/02)**

PLAYIN' QPR AWAY and Brett Angel gets booked and the whole Blues End bursts into, "Off! Off! Off!" Doubled me up. Later on Nev is taking a run up for a goal kick when someone shouts, "Don't fuckin' aim for Angel!" Big Nev pissed himself and had to take his run up again. **Gal (06/05/02)**

DURING THE BLACKBURN DEFEAT on Sunday the Street End were giving Paul Gerrard loads — sarcastically clapping when he caught anything, when some fella goes, "Ignore them, Gezza — you're going to Korea ... Let's hope you don't come back." **Robbie G (03/05/02)**

DURING A BAD SPELL John Ebbrell was having at the club, in one game he committed a bad foul, and was about to be lectured by the ref, when chants came from our supporters, "Off, off, off!" Both funny and sad at the same time. **Allan Baall (10/01/02)**

MY FAVOURITE COMMENT was at the League Cup tie at Forest in 1989 (the one we lost after Big Nev was penalised for steps). A young boy on the row in front was asking about Neil Pointon. "Why's he called Dissa, Dad?" "Because he's crap, son," was the reply. **Alex May (10/01/02)**

AT THE RECENT UNITED GAME, Rhino missed a sitter at the end of the first half, when some old guy shouted, "Fuck off, Rhino, you're shite. You couldn't hit a cow's arse with a banjo." Which was quickly replied with, "He couldn't hit his own arse with a banjo." Classic. **David McWilliam (10/01/02)**

WE WENT TO WATCH a pre-season friendly between Bangor and Marine a few years ago when Graeme Sharp was their manager. We got there a little bit late but suddenly noticed that Bangor's number 10 was a bit weighty. As the game went on we noticed it was none other than Sharpy himself. The four of us starting singing, "Sharpy, Sharpy, give us a wave!" to which he obliged. As he was a little past his heyday, he was constantly offside. Bangor started another offensive to which one of the lads shouted, "Breathe in Sharpy, you're offside!" Good on him though ... he did an over-exaggerated 'breathe in' and gave us another wave! What a bloke! **Robbie G (10/01/02)**

AT THE CHARLTON GAME Alexandersson falls on to the ground yet again when up comes the shout, "Hey! Alexandersson! No wonder they call you 'Lino', you're always on the floor." **Ian Macdonald (31/12/01)**

AT THE SOUTHAMPTON GAME on the 2 December and we played the usual dismal first half. Some fella shouts, "What's that Smith doing? He's only playing one fella in the correct position – and that's fuckin' Gerrard on the bench." **Parkend 121 (30/12/01)**

MAIN STAND – Tranmere debacle – during the prolonged silence after Tranmere's third. "Why don't you fuck off, Smith? You're just Gordon Lee in a fucking kilt." **Dixies Leg (04/10/01)**

ANOTHER ONE was when Paul Rideout got that pretty bad head injury on the half-way line, he had a lot of stitches in his mouth and lost a tooth. The next home game, Joe Royle took to his seat in the dugout and the bloke behind me asked Joe how Rideout was. Joe replied, "He will be alright, he's had a cap on his tooth." The reply came swiftly from behind, "It's the only cap he's ever got." **Duggy (19/12/01)**

I THINK IT WAS '95 and Joe 'The Pieman' Parkinson was having a stinker. After a particularly shite pass, the bloke in front stands up and exclaims, "Parkinson ... you're a fucking disease!" Quality. **Paul Feenan (04/10/01)**

THE FELLA WHO SITS BEHIND ME in the Upper Gwladys is a pearl. This season's gems from his gob include, "Get your haircut, Campbell," after he failed to latch on to a through ball. And, "With tackles like that we know why the buffalo is extinct," to David Unsworth. It was then pointed out to him that Unsworth is known as Rhino, "They're both the same," was the reply. **Derek Wadeson (27/09/01)**

AT THE PALACE GAME last week, Chadwick had a weak shot at the keeper, to which the guy behind me shouted, "Cadamateri hit his tart harder than that!" **the jiggerrabbit (21/09/01)**

ONE OF MY FAVOURITES has to be from the early 80s. Whenever Billy Wright got the ball, the bloke behind me in the Street End always tried to help by shouting, "Blue Shirt, Billy!" **Joe Baker (20/09/01)**

IN THE PARK END, after Dave Unsworth had cleared off the line, the chant of, "Rhino, Rhino" came from the Street End. The kid behind me asked, "Why do they call him Rhino, Dad?" Simple reply, "Cos he's got an arse like yer ma's, lad." **Lard (19/09/01)**

SCOTT GEMMILL, having one of his shockingly, piss poor experiences in a blue shirt. An arl man in front of me stands up and shouts, "Gemmill, if your arl fella was dead, he'd be rolling in his fucking coffin." **Ste Flynn (24/09/03)**

PLAYING CHELSEA AT HOME, 2-0 down after half an hour and we're getting restless in the Upper Bullens. Graveson was having his normal headless chicken game. After his shot at goal had gone just wide, the Gwladys Street started chanting his name. As he's running back into the centre circle he puts his hands up and claps back to the fans. Bloke behind me shouts out, "Somebody throw the twat a fish." That even got some of the old dears in the Upper Bullens laughing. **Phil Armand (21/12/02)**

AWAY AT CHELSEA last season and Franny 'jug-ears' Jeffers warms up right in front of the travelling Blues. He's getting some serious abuse after his outburst against Moyesy. Anyway, he's standing next to this linesman who has similarly shaped ears to Franny. Some fella shouts out, "Fuck off you, yer big-eared twat." So this linesman starts waggling his ears when some other fella shouts, "Not you, linesman ... yer big-eared twat." Everyone was in stitches. **Thornton Toffee Chris (16/08/04)**

FIRST GAME OF THE SEASON against Aston Villa and Pembridge's first corner was welcomed by, "Fuck off, you, you've done fuck all, all season." **Tom Rowe (02/10/02)**

AT BORO GAME on Saturday during a dire first half, some guy behind me in Park End shouts, "C'mon, Tie, get into the game." Which was quickly followed up by someone else shouting, "Aye, and get a fucking hair cut while you're at it." **James T (22/09/02)**

JUST BEFORE THE KENDALL GLORY YEARS began, Gary Stanley was not having the best of times of it at Goodison. I was in Goodison Road in a smallish crowd and Stanley was having a nightmare. The crowd was on his back and he deserved it. The ball came out for a throw-in near where I was standing and Stan came over to take it. The guy next to me shouted out, "Hey! Stan! I backed you to score the first goal." Stan visibly glowed with delight until, with perfect timing, the fan shouted, "Yeah, I got two thousand to one!" **Fernsy (09/12/02)**

WHEN PAUL GERRARD was down injured on the ground and Paolo Di Canio caught the ball. Me arl fella shouted, "Don't help 'im, just dig 'im in." **Rob (19/11/02)**

IT WAS AT THE FULHAM GAME this season and when we were 2-0 up we were doing fine. Unsy then plays a perfect ball through to Pembridge who only has 10 yards to cover to reach it and Zat Knight has about 30 yards to cover to reach it. Knight gets to the ball before Pembridge and some disabled guy shouts, "Come on, Pembridge! I'm in a wheelchair, and even I could have reached that." Brilliant. **Rob (01/11/02)**

A COUPLE OF SEASONS AGO when we had Paul Gascoigne pulling the strings in midfield, can't remember who we were playing but it was the usual shite we had to put up with when Smith was in charge. Arse end of the game and on comes our Israeli supersub Idan Tal when a lad in our row says, "Tal's only come to Everton because he wants Gazza's strip!" Jeremy Paxman meets the Upper Gwladys. **Treax (31/10/04)**

EXCLUSIVE GRAEME SHARP INTERVIEW

FRIDAY 8 DECEMBER 2000. Blue Kipper were honoured and privileged to meet up with and interview Everton legend, Graeme Sharp, using questions posted to the site. The meeting with Everton's post-war record goalscorer took place in the EFC Restaurant at Goodison Park.

BK: Graeme, what made you choose Everton?

GS: As a player I had the choice of a number of clubs. My brother was the talk of Rangers and Celtic but had had a number of bad experiences which my father wanted me to avoid by going to a smaller club. I went to Dumbarton. Chances came to move to Aberdeen and Aston Villa where I had been on trial for a week, but nothing had materialised. I then came down with my father to Everton to meet Gordon Lee and the Secretary Jim Greenwood. We had lunch (in here as it happens). I was still a young lad thinking I was just there to be shown around. They showed me a fantastic stadium, fantastic training ground and then offered there and then to sign me. It was a big, big step for me, but having been in Scotland and knowing Everton were a big club in English football, I could relate to Everton, the fact that they had players like Bob Latchford and Asa Hartford, a Scottish international, it was very important to me to come down to a big club. It was a big step in my career, I could have stayed in Scotland, but when I came down and saw the place it took my breath away. Even things like restaurants inside the ground, which at the time I did not think existed! Gordon Lee was very focused and he looked after me in those early days. People have differing opinions of him, but I found him a to be a good man. I've seen his look-a-like on the bluekipper site and the less said about that the better!

BK: Have you always had the competitive streak in you?

GS: My father always said that I did not have enough belief in myself. When I first came down playing alongside Steve McMahon, Joe McBride, Paul Lodge – all good players – I thought to myself, even though I'd signed for £125,000, that I wasn't good enough and perhaps shouldn't be here. I was shy, retiring and not at all pushy. I had a bit of an inferiority complex when I first arrived. It was only after working with and talking to Colin Harvey that things changed. I was in the last year of my contract, it was make or break and my father told me to go and show them what I could do. Working with Colin and alongside Andy you learnt how to look after yourself. You needed a passion and desire to win and I had that. You needed that to succeed at the top level, particularly in the striking position.

BK: Can we go back to the aggression bit, you and Andy Gray, how did it rub off on you?

GS: Colin or Howard had told me not to get brushed off the ball and Andy had the approach of, "Don't let anybody effin' boss you about," and it went from there. Take the games against Spurs, Roberts and Miller, it was like World War Two kicking lumps out of each other. My Dad always said, "Don't let anyone ever bully you – always get your retaliation in first." I always tell the tale about one of my first games here against Leeds, Kenny Burns was centre half and fearsome, his first words were something like, "I'm going to break your effin' leg …" I thought that's out of order, my old fella's words are ringing in my ear when I get a chance and give it to him on the half-way line, ball ends up out for a corner to us and Kenny is out for the count getting smelling salts on the half-way line. I thought he's going to kill me here but he was as quiet as a mouse. We won 1-0 and I scored. If someone kicked me, I kicked them back, I could play it either way.

BK: As a kid, a number of top clubs were after you. Were you on Celtic's books?

GS: No, Celtic Amateurs then Eastercraigs. Not Celtic, as I am
        Rangers, although my son supports Everton and Celtic!

BK: How badly did you upset Ron Saunders by not signing for Villa
        and were there any later repercussions?

GS: No, not really, I went there for a week's trial. Andy Gray and
        Brian Little were there. Andy was a hero of mine, he doesn't
        like me saying that, but he was and Villa were a big club. I'd
        been down for a trial as a fifteen-year-old and nothing
        materialised, but now I was older and had been at
        Dumbarton for a year. I did well and was called in by Mr
        Saunders along with my then manager, Davie Wilson, and a
        director, Sean Fallon. He said I'd done well but there was no
        offer of a signing. I came back up, I would have liked to sign
        for Villa but then Gordon Lee came up to see me in a Tuesday
        night match in which I scored, but we lost and the phone went
        the following morning inviting me down to Everton. After I'd
        signed the forms, articles appeared in the paper saying Ron
        Saunders had gone mad as he had been gazumped. I scored
        plenty of goals later against Villa in my career but there was
        no animosity. I know I was fortunate to choose Everton ahead
        of Aston Villa.

BK: When did your love affair with the fans begin and how did it
        grow after 'that' goal at Anfield?

GS   It was difficult for me at first being homesick and only getting
        a few first team opportunities at the end of the season. I
        thought the fans didn't fancy me as a player and things were
        slow to happen. In the dark days of '83 opinion was varied
        on me and it was a hard time. Believe me, seven thousand
        fans at Goodison can be a scary experience when you can
        spot everyone in the crowd and everyone is having a go at
        you! As soon as they saw the change in the team you could
        almost sense something was going to happen. I always
        believed that if you showed passion, commitment and worked
        hard, that the fans would take to you. I say that to everyone
        that comes here.

BK: Was the half-time talk in the Bayern Munich game to basically
        kick shit out of them in the second half?

GS: (after laughing) No, I've said before Howard just said to keep
        it going. When we went 0-1 down the silence was
        unbelievable; it was eerie in what was an unbelievable
        atmosphere. Howard said that the Street End would suck one
        in, as it happened the first goal came off my eyebrow, I think.
        Having been battered over there with a depleted side we rode
        our luck at times and came away with a 0-0 draw. So coming
        back here with everybody fit we knew we could turn them over,
        we knew we'd also have a crowd of fifty thousand behind us,
        so we had a great lift. We'd arrive at the ground by coach
        from a hotel in town, usual routine, except this night when the
        coach turned towards the ground it came to a standstill. We
        could not believe it and it then sunk in how big this was. You
        could always hear the crowd but this was a different buzz, we
        believed in ourselves and just wanted to get stuck into the
        Germans. Andy's goal followed mine and Trevor rounded it
        off. It was a great day. I remember Hoeness chasing Andy
        down the tunnel at the end and Andy coming out with the
        proverbial, "F off. We're in the final and you're not." But,
        make no mistake, they gave as good as they got in what was
        a physical battle which at the end of the day we won.

BK: How did the mood of the players and Club change after the
        Heysel incident resulting in the European ban?

GS: People were talking about us going on and dominating Europe
        and we were looking forward to it. As a player you want to
        reach the pinnacle of the European Cup. Sadly it was taken
        away from us through no fault of our own. We were
        disappointed, but you look to all the people that died, that was
        a sad thing for football. Who knows, we may have been drawn
        against Real Madrid in the first round, but we really did fancy
        our chances. It subsequently resulted in Trevor and Gary
        going, there was the lure of European football and the money
        being paid at Rangers. Howard left and was successful at
        Bilbao, Andy Gray went to accommodate Links, which I
        thought was a wrong move. Whilst me and Links scored a lot
        of goals, I was looking forward to renewing my partnership
        with Andy. But these decisions have to be made and not
        everyone connected to the football club likes them.

BK: Andy was one of your heroes, is that why you two were the only ones wearing white socks with black shoes at the evening celebration following the '84 Cup Final?

GS: Not me, Andy was a fashion victim, mine were light grey!

BK: Right on the spot now – in the past you usually name four goals as your best ever – Wembley '84, Spurs '82, Sheffield Wednesday semi '86 and, of course, THE one against the Shite. Come down off the fence, which was the best ?

GS: For being spectacular and more difficult, the Spurs one was the hardest to execute. The best would have to be that one against them – it was spectacular, it was against them, it was the first time we had won there in thirteen years and we went on to win the Championship. Also, for the fellow who ran on the pitch, who for a long time I thought was the fellow who cleaned my windows after I heard a story that got mixed up. Then I went to a dinner last year and met this shy lad sat in the corner who proved it was him and I realised that I'd had the wrong bloke, my window cleaner, for years!

BK: What was the story behind you missing out on the England v Scotland international?

GS: I got twelve Scotland caps but never played against England, I played twelve times in which they never lost a game. I was called up for the game where Goughie scored the header and we won 1-0 at Hampden, where I was down to play. Jock Stein got a call on the Friday and I was pulled to one side. Everton were playing Coventry on the Sunday and Coventry were involved in a relegation scrap. Fellow relegation candidates complained they would be playing a weakened side, so I was called back and missed out. It was a horrible weekend for me – we got battered 4-1 – and it is one of my great regrets that I never played in a Scotland v England game.

BK: Many Merseysiders were howling laughing recently when you discussed your role as Fans' Liaison Officer with an angry fan on the post match phone-in after the derby – it was hilarious. What is your role and job description?

GS: People say to me, "What is it that the Fans' Liaision Officer actually does?" I don't think any other club has one. Alan

Myers approached me and asked me for a recommendation of an ex-Everton player who could do the job, I couldn't, but said that I would be interested, had it not been for other commitments. He then phoned me asking to meet Michael Dunford, so I did. The role was described as a link between the Club and the fans. It involves a lot of charity work – cancer charities, hospital liaision and supporters' clubs – the Club wants to build closer links with all their fans. A figurehead for the Club representing Everton and gaining good PR, the role is difficult to define. That fan wanted me here when I was working elsewhere. I am there with the team witnessing live events such as recently at Sunderland. I do enjoy the role. Another example was the day when I had been with a family spreading ashes at Goodison.

BK: As Fans' Liaision Officer don't you think a fan who knows the A-Z of being a supporter, just as you know the Club inside out, should be appointed to work alongside you? PS I know of thirty thousand applicants!

GS: I get good feedback from fans on a regular basis, don't get me wrong, it may be an idea, but I don't know if Bill has any plans.

BK: What is the truth behind Joe Parkinson going?

GS: Joe always said he wanted to work in a different line – he gave it ten weeks. He had just come from football where the hours are completely different, going from having almost the whole day to yourself to nine to five plus. He also has a young family, so I think there are personal reasons as well.

BK: Who was the hardest – Keown or Sheedy?

GS: In that instance, Keown, but let's just say that the man who has been drinking Coke all day will always win!

BK: In one particular derby incident you were involved with Jan Molby and both elbows were used. What was all that about and what did Molby say?

GS: Darren Coyle had had his leg broken in the mini-derby by a naughty challenge. Big Jan had said some unsavoury things that had boiled tempers even more. So, as you do on those occasions, I made sure that Jan knew I was unhappy with what he had said.

BK: When you were involved in the Chris Fairclough 'Kirkby kiss' incident, Cloughie was hopping mad. Were there any repercussions in the tunnel, or afterwards?

GS: I love it when it kicks off because they are concentrating on me instead of the game. Usual Cloughie stuff after the game: "Young man ..." We'd won 5-0 and I scored two. We had a return late in the season and I was in the dugout with Sheeds, Reidy, Brace and Andy being rested. Teams come out and Cloughie marches towards the dugout. I thought, this should be interesting. He says, "Young man, it's a good job you are not playing today."
"Why's that?"
"Because I told my son Nigel to kick your ..."
"Your son Nigel! Do me a favour! Fuck off! I'm not afraid of your son Nigel. We've got a Cup Winners' Cup Final next week."
"Quite right too, young man, and all the best in the final!"
He was off his trolley!

BK: You played under Sir Alex for Scotland, what did you think of him then and did your opinion change after he slagged you off in his book regarding the Uruguay game?

GS: No, he wanted to sign me on three occasions; at Dumbarton he wanted to take me to St Mirren; at Everton he wanted to take me to Aberdeen a couple of times. He had a reputation as a bully, giving you the 'hair drier treatment' right in your face. I'd heard stories from the Aberdeen lads and didn't fancy working for anyone like that. Then I went to play for Scotland when he took over from Jock Stein and I had no problems. Then he goes and writes something like that in the book. What he is forgetting is that he has to live with his own performance and in those three World Cup games – he failed. That year I'd scored thirty-one goals with Links and Frank McAvennie had scored about twenty-nine with West Ham with Tony Cottee. Charlie Nicholas had scored about three for Arsenal and Paul Sturrock a few for Dundee United. A manager needs to make decisions. First game I'm not involved, not even in the sixteen, we got beat. Same again for the second game, my involvement was collecting the balls after training and doing my own thing. Then comes the third game, they realise they must win, I'm called into the team, not having been involved in any of the tactics or training with the first team squad and he decides to play with no wingers! I was criticised for not being aggressive enough in the box, but he dropped Davie Cooper and there were no crosses. He also dropped Graeme Souness, against Uruguay, of all teams, in a game where everybody thought he would be ideal against their hard men. The rest is history. I was involved in the Scottish team that took the only point in the World Cup. It's easy to criticise me along with the likes of Brian Kidd and Gordon Strachan, but if he looks at it deep down, he was the one who made mistakes. The job at the time was probably too much for him. He's now gone on to great things and all credit to him.

BK: Where does Marshall – your middle name – come from?

GS: I think it's from my father's side somewhere. There are no links between this and wearing the cowboy hat and carrying the gun for the Echo photo when I first arrived!

BK: At which hairdressers did you get your hair permed in the eighties, and which players resisted the temptation?

GS: It was a mad spell and it wasn't a perm it was a demi-wave! I think I went up to Scotland to have it done originally, then I went somewhere in Church Street – the less said the better. I don't like reminders. I wasn't alone – Inchy and Kevin Rich had one and, of course, John Bailey's was natural and before us there was Latch and Georgie Wood.

BK: Your best man was Kevin Richardson. Do you still see him and what is he up to?

GS: I see him now and again at foundation dinners and on holiday a few years ago, but not as much as I'd like. Kev's back now working for Sunderland with the academy. He was only a bit part player here, a very good one, he moved on to have a great career at Villa, Coventry, Arsenal and over in Sociadad. He's done very well for himself.

BK: He played in a great game at Anfield, for Arsenal.

GS: What a wonderful game, we were in Magaluf, in a bar, which lost the picture and had commentary only. It was fabulous, we had been there all day and when the second goal went in it was an excuse for a party. When we got back and saw the Steve McMahon one-minute finger it made it all the better.

BK: Do you keep in touch with your ex-striking partner Gary Lineker and is he the little shit we all think he is?

GS: I saw Links last year when I did a bit on Football Focus. Links was alright here, no problems in the dressing room, he mixed and his goal scoring record was good. I've got no gripes, even though people say I made him a millionaire when he went to Barcelona, but he was a better player when he came back. What sticks in people's throats, I think, is that when he mentions his ex-clubs he seems to have little affinity with Everton, but I still think he holds Everton close, even though he doesn't show it. No, he doesn't send me a Christmas card, unlike Andy and Mike Newall.

BK: Apparently, you passed your driving test late in life. When? Who used to take you to training and matches?

GK: About 1992, I'd had enough getting the train from Southport to Oldham and the wife had had enough as well. I've cadged a lift off loads of people: Sheeds, Andy, Alan Irvine, Ian Snodin. It was laziness, but the bargain was that you could have a drink.

BK: Would you stick with the current team (okay, we lost one on Monday) or would you revert to the pre-season big money signings?

GS: Difficult, given how well they have done, but a manager must stick with the side he knows is his best.

BK: Did you have a dislike not only for the Shite but particularly Steve Nicol?

GS: No, not Stevie Nic, we got on well. Don't get me wrong, we would kick each other, maybe you are getting mixed up with Steve McMahon, as we both wanted to win so badly. I hated losing, particularly against them. It made it even worse – I even go there now and it pains me, I can't stand them.

BK: Colin Harvey worked for you at Oldham, was it difficult telling him what to do?

GS: No, because I never did. I have great respect for him, Colin helped me in a coaching capacity, as he is qualified. Unfortunately it was at the wrong time, Oldham having been relegated and lacking ambition as a club.

BK: Many people feel you left Everton too soon, indeed you went on to prove them right. Did you ever ask Howard why he sold you?

GS: Not really, no. A manager makes a decision and has to live with it, but I found it farcical at the time. A friend approached me on holiday in America with the missus and kids and asked if I would fancy going to Oldham. I told him to get lost. I came back from holiday and at pre-season training Howard called me in and accused me of speaking to Joe Royle, which I denied. He told me he was thinking of bringing Dean Saunders in and I said I was willing to fight for my place. Howard said he had sorted something with Joe. I asked him to phone and cancel, which he wouldn't. I met up with Joe and told him straight I didn't wish to go. Howard clearly did not want me and said Everton could not match Oldham's offer. I felt that I had served the Club for eleven years and the whole thing could have been handled much better. It was a sad time. They got five hundred thousand for me when I never wanted to leave.

BK: Remember the eighties programmes with the player and wife centrefold? Who supplied the Val Doonican sweaters you all wore?

GS: Shows how much football has moved on, it was always bad photos then, I remember the cowboy one and another with Sheeds with a clarinet and me with a trumpet, ridiculous! That dog that was in the picture, my pet, bit me once before the Notts Forest game. I was clowning around with him around Christmas time, rolling around on the floor and he was growling. The wife warned me and the next thing he bit through my hand. We were due to play on the Sunday and I phoned Clinks (John Clinkard – physio) after I'd been to hospital for treatment and told him I couldn't play the next day as the dog had bitten me, and I'd had stitches and my hand was like a balloon. Clinks called me straight in, I looked like the Mummy, my hand was twice its normal size, so I couldn't play. Wayne Clarke came in for me, scored, and we won 1-0!

BK: What is it really like to score the winning goal in the derby. We've all done it, but usually at 3am then woken up in a damp patch?

GS: Everyone talks to me about this, that day at Anfield, I don't know why. I ran to the crowd, everyone knows about the guy who ran on, but I fixed on the crowd and saw a guy called Eddide Done – a mad Evertonian and a friend of Colin Harvey. I still see him to this day. I just locked on to him. To see those faces in the crowd, it is just fantastic.

BK: Best striking partner?

GS: For goalscoring, Lineker. I enjoyed playing with Inchy, but in terms of winning and physical enjoyment it has to be Andy Gray. There was talk of pairing up with Rushy at Juventus – that would have been interesting. I also would have liked to play alongside Bob Latchford for longer.

BK: And the worst?

GS: Mick Ferguson, Alan Biley, Rob Wakenshaw. There were a few lazy ones including Tony Cottee. If we'd lost and he'd scored, he felt it was job done, whilst muggins here was running all over the park. In his book he says people did not pass to him at Goodison – load of tripe – it was him who did not give enough to the team.

BK: Fittest players at the Club?

GS: Gary Stevens and Pat Van Den Hauwe (even after a night out).

BK: Best centre half opponent?

GS: David O'Leary – you could never get at him even physically – quick and a good reader of the game.

BK: Best player you played with at Everton?

GS: Some would say Trevor, but from my view it was Sheeds because I knew what he was going to do. If he pulled it on to his left foot he was going for the diagonal ball and I would peel off and get to the back post.

BK: How did you feel when you went around Grobbellar at Anfield and missed?

GS: Bloody awful. I was never great one-on-one. I was more instictive. Training with Nev made one-on-ones almost impossible.

BK: Twenty-sixth March1988, you were captain for the last time, is it right you got the coin from the ref?

GS: No, I remember the game and think it was the one and only time I was captain. It was a great honour for me but I never received the coin, referees are too tight for that.

BK: Have you ever thought of managing the Blues?

GS: I'd love to, but I think that's past now. Oldham didn't work out, and I'm just happy to be back at the Club.

BK: Recent times have not been good for the Club, we recognise that there have been many positive changes over the last couple of years. Have we turned the corner and how long before we are challenging for honours?

GS: I think it is difficult with Man U, Arsenal and Leeds ahead of us, just look across the park where they have invested over sixty million and I don't see a good side there. I think with our financial problems it will be difficult for us over the next two to three years, but hopefully we are moving the right way. This was one of the reasons I came back. I believe the Club is in the right hands, we have a fabulous fan base, football is an up-and-coming business and there is more to be had out there. I still think, I said it years ago, there are three priorities, the ground, the academy and the team on the pitch, whatever way you want to approach this depends. all the top teams have this right, I see the Academy as the future of the Club and we need to address this, but it is only one part. We've got the Manager right and hopefully with more backing we will see that you couldn't get a better man for the job.

BK: On behalf of all at Blue Kipper and all other Blues I'd like to say thank you for all that you've done for us. Thankyou, Graeme Sharp.

I'LL GET ME COAT

Whether it's the heat of the moment, the pre-match ale, or just because some of us are unbelievably thick, we keep saying things we wish we hadn't.

THIS LINK IS VERY IRONIC. First home game of the season sitting in the Park End against Fulham. Joey Yobo goes up for a header in the first half after a corner and makes a complete mess of it. Me arl fella shouts, "Campbell, you're fucking rubbish." To which I hear laughter from the rows in front and the only reply, "Shut up, you prick," – a very embarrassed season ticket holder. **Mally (12/09/03)**

MY MATE MATT was at the Man City game three weeks ago and the fans were giving us loads when he shouted, "I fucking hate these fans more than I hate Mancs." The bottom seven rows were in stitches. Great times. **Jay Size (10/10/04)**

LAST SEASON I went the match with two mates. It was against Fulham and we were right behind the goal. Me mate stands up and shouts, "Van der Sar! yer French bastard!" Everyone turns around an' he goes, "I mean Italian." So about three or four men turn round and say, "He's Dutch, mate." **Joey Willo (15/07/04)**

BACK IN '97 AT A MANC GAME at Goodison, sittin' in Upper Gwladys, some nasty tackles flyin' in around the centre of the park. Fat lad behind us shouts … "Oi! Roy Keane! You dirty bastard, I fuckin' hate you! … You're not even Roy Keane, are you? You sneaky little bastard!" Had us all in stitches. **Ian (27/01/05)**

GOING BACK YEARS, about '94. We were playin' Leeds who at the time weren't all that good, but then again, neither were we. Anyway, it was a dull 0-0 game when some arl fella bout 80 who never said a word, just kicked off for ten minutes using, "Shite, garbage, bollocks an' bring Ferguson on," every other sentence. The steward come over, and we thought he was gonner get kicked out, he just said, "Sit down mate, Ferguson started." Funny shit. **Keebs (13/11/02)**

I WAS SITTING IN THE UPPER BULLENS some time ago, watching the worst match ever, against Luton (I think it may have been the last before the Street End was seated, but I digress). Feeling extremely annoyed as our former USA, 5-a-side player fell over once again. I finally lost my patience and shouted, "Oh! Prickie! you fucking prek!" Needless to say, I felt like a right prek. **Richie (10/06/03)**

WE WERE SITTING watching the teams warm up before the dire Fulham farce, when some geezer shouts to Simmonsen, "Hey! lad! You weren't to blame for the Shrewsbury game." To which Steve replies, "Of course I wasn't, I didn't play." Cue red-faced fan and the rest of us pissing ourselves laughing at him. **Neil Davies (09/05/03)**

IN THE PARK END on Saturday against the Hammers, ref, Mark Halsey, having another sub-standard game, blows for something and gives a free kick to Joe Cole. A shout from behind, "Halsey, I hope your dog dies." Followed with an apology to those people surrounding, "I had to say something and it's what came into my head. I like dogs." It sort of summed up the game. **Mark (03/04/03)**

MICKEY MOUSE CUP GAME this season against Charlton. One of their players goes down injured and the keeper kicks the ball into the family enclosure. Some feller gives him the finger for kicking it at the crowd but his missus turns round and gives him a clip round the head and plenty of earache. Everyone was in stitches, including their goalie. **Thomas (09/01/04)**

I WAS SAT WITH MY DAD and uncle in the Upper Bullens at the Villa game (2003), just behind the camera stand. The bloke in front of us sees an Everton sub warming up. He lets of out a cry of relief, "Thank God, Yobo is coming on!" Only problem was that it was as clear as day that it was actually Duncan Ferguson, pointed out to him by numerous fans around him. Quality. **Paul B (22/10/03)**

BACK IN THE NOT-SO-TERRIFIC 1993/94 season, I forget the game, I was in the Lower Bullens, and about half way through the first half a fella jumped up (and in the hope of starting a chant) shouted, "We are Everton." His only reaction being a fat git about 6 rows forward turning round and shouting, "Don't fucking remind us." Superb. **EFC Forever (10/05/02)**

I SIT BEHIND THE BENCH in the Family Enclosure and there's a bloke in front of me with a Chris Woods fixation. Every time Gerrard fucks up, he starts shouting, "Eh! Woods! Woods! You useless bastard. What do you get paid for, eh, Woods? Sitting there on your arse every week. Goalkeeping coach are yer? What do you do with him all week, eh?" He blames Woods for every single mistake Gerrard makes! As you can imagine, this lad was in Woods overdrive on Saturday against the Geordies, but he wasn't too happy when following a crucial second half Gerrard save, me arl fella shouted, "Nice one, Woods, keep it up lad!" **Ben Fardey (31/10/01)**

A FEW SEASONS AGO when we were playing Spurs at home, after a bit of shit midfield play the ball falls to Chris Armstrong, some fella jumps up and shouts, "Don't worry, he's shite." And what does he do? Puts it over Big Nev's head and into the back of the net. **Big Dunk (06/04/02)**

A FEW OF US WENT OVER for our annual defeat at Tranmere last year and we could only get in the Tranmere End. As you know, them knobheads haven't got a clue, but on this occasion I had a chuckle. They were singing, "If you all hate Scousers clap your hands." To which my fat mate shouted back on his own, "Sheep, sheep, sheep shaggers." Imagine his face when the whole end turned around and sang, "Who ate all the pies?" and "You fat bastard," and "Are you Gazza in disguise?" – just to him. Class. **Mark (20/02/02)**

AT THE ARSENAL GAME this season. Whoever was right back (I think it was Upson) got injured and went off, then Lee Dixon came on to replace. The same Lee Dixon that has played right back for Arsenal for 10 years+. Then some guy in front of me shouts, "This is alright, that's Dixon playing right back, he's out of position." **Stephen Hope (22/03/02)**

TOTTENHAM GAME this season when a frustrated bloke behind me shouts, "Take Li Tie off." His mate replies, "He's gone off." To which this bloke responds, "Then take him off again!" **Simon's Dad (27/12/02)**

EXCLUSIVE KEVIN RATCLIFFE INTERVIEW

WE MET EVERTON'S MOST SUCCESFUL CAPTAIN in his manager's office at Shrewsbury Town Football Club. We asked him the questions you sent to Blue Kipper. Plus a few of our own. We had a half hour appointment. We stayed for two hours. Here are Kevin's answers.

BK: I'm a South Waleian Blue, Kevin, and I'd like to ask you about your reaction on your debut when you scored for Cardiff, you went nuts and ran fifty yards after you scored, was it as good as scoring against the Red Shite?

KR: A goal's a goal for me, it was only my third ever. I didn't know how to celebrate and when you score on your debut ... particularly as I'd supposedly finished playing. It was quite a good end to my career that year as we won the Championship with Cardiff. And no, it wasn't quite as good as scoring against the Red Shite.

BK: How much did you pay Bruce Grobbellar to let 'that goal' in?

KR: I wasn't asked to go to court, so I must have been alright.

BK: Do you ever get asked that question since Bruce's case?

KR: What do you mean, "Since the case?" It was said at the time! When you know Bruce, nothing surprises you, but the shot did have a bit of swerve on it at the end! It wouldn't have mattered if Nev had been in, he still wouldn't have got it!

BK: How did you come to be spotted by Everton as a kid?

KR: A chap called Ryan from St Asaph watched me play and asked if I wanted to go for a trial. I was playing for Flintshire Boys and I think they wanted to sign me. I started training at Everton and playing for the A and B teams. However, I was also playing for Chester Youth as Chester were also interested. I knew most of the lads at Chester as they were all local. It was a toss up between the two clubs as to who I signed for. The set up at Everton, particularly for a young lad, was unbelievable. The frightening part was that you would not make the team until you were twenty, or twenty-one. Whereas, at Chester, you could be in the team at sixteen or seventeen, playing regularly like Rushy. Everton had the pull because I used to go and watch them and everyone in our house was brought up as an Evertonian.

BK: How long did you have to wait before you made your first team debut?

KR: I was nineteen and made my debut at Man United in front of fifty-eight thousand. John Gidman went down ill and it was sprung on me in the afternoon. I moved to centre back and Billy Wright went to right back – 12 March 1980 – we drew 0-0. My second game was the FA Cup semi against West Ham at Elland Road. I wasn't even in the squad for the first game. Kiddo gets sent off, on the Monday I'm in the squad and Wednesday I'm playing! It was a big disappointment, with one exception, I was over the moon, I'd played in a semi-final and got three times my wage on appearance. Looking around the dressing room and on the coach, people like Peter Eastoe, Latchy and Mick Lyons were crying, saying, "You've got plenty of time to get to another final, we'll not get another chance." They were quite right.

BK: With all due respect to the greatest captain in Everton's history, how come you were outstanding in the middle and crap at left-back?

KR: You may have a point. Early on in your career you just want to play and you'll play anywhere. I didn't really enjoy left-back until late on in my career. I played a dozen or so late on at Everton and thoroughly enjoyed it. I was more experienced,

95

was comfortable on the ball, unlike those early days. I was brought on as a midfield/centre back. Some might cringe at the thought of midfield! I never saw myself as a left-back and had the argument with Howard, who told me to get in the pecking order. For example, he wouldn't play me and Mark Higgins together as we were two left-footers. I got my chance when Billy Wright was dropped after I kept feeding him a few pies!

BK: Around this time there was a rumour that Bobby Robson wanted you at Ipswich, was that right?

KR: So I believe, along with Stoke and Blackburn, but I never even spoke to them. Howard told me at the PFA awards that Stoke were after me. I said, "Are they?" and Howard said, "Yes, I've told them to fuck off," which was nice to hear.

BK: So Howard was a good man manager?

KR: Oh, Yes. Not only was he a good man manager, but people forget that he returned as player manager and I played in the same side as him. You don't realise, as a supporter, how good a player he was. He was always first pick on the five-a-side at training because he never gave the ball away. The training was superb, he knew what the lads wanted, he worked on the back four and that was a first for me. It was, "This is what we want", "Squeeze up, hold the line and mark space". We always marked space, never man-marked. Howard was good, very good.

BK: Something else the fans remember more fondly, often with a few beers down us and the video on, is the Bayern Munich game. In particular, the tackle early in the second half on Ludwig Kogl. Do you recall it?

KR: I was just one of a few of us out for the dangerman. I didn't even get booked, I always said sorry. Early on I used to walk away, then one season I got more bookings than Frank Sinatra, so I started to say sorry. Howard pointed Kogl out as the dangerman and that was enough, you may as well have put a target on his kneecap, ankle or calf!

BK: It was his thigh I seem to remember?

KR: Well isn't that where your thighs are – around by your bollocks? Me and Reidy said we'd sort him out. Having said that, Reidy had six or seven stitches in a gash that night, which people don't realise. He ran over to the bench and shoved a wet sponge down his sock and never went off for stitches. It was Lother Matthias that did it. At the same time, Andy back-headed their centre half who had about twenty stitches in a nose, face and lip wound! They said to Howard, that their bench could not believe what was going on. "Mr Kendall, this is not football." Howard turned around and said, "Fuck off!"

BK: What other memories do you have of that night?

KR: Biggest game of my career. We dare not lose. Fifty thousand Evertonians and about a thousand of theirs. We couldn't even get near the stadium in the bus. We were late. The whole build-up was so emotional (similar to Wimbledon, but for different reasons). The atmosphere at night is even more highly charged.

BK: Strong rumours are that you are a good friend of David Moyes and you are returning as his number two?

KR: I'm not a good friend, I know him and there has not been any approach. I've known Dave a while as we used to holiday in the same resort and have a drink together, this was whilst he was just the coach at Preston. I'm made up with his appointment at Everton. I've never applied, or been approached by Everton. Of course, once an Evertonian, always an Evertonian, and you want to manage at the highest level. It would be nice to get the chance!

BK: How do you think Moysey will do?

KR: It's going to be a hard job – it would be for anyone because the money situation is not the greatest. Teams bring in £4million players for the bench, Everton would need to play that type of player week in and week out and that's the sad thing about it, they are no longer the big club that they were.

By that I mean no longer a big spending club. It is a fantastic, massive club, but so are Villa and they spend more than Everton. In the past we were always up there – Lineker, Watson, Cottee – all record deals, but we don't see that anymore, we can't compete with Man United, Leeds, Arsenal and Chelsea. It's a shame because there are Evertonians all over the world.

BK: Did any game ever come near the Bayern Munich game?

KR: Well, obviously, the Cup Finals, but for me personally, it was a comeback game against Wimbledon. The Press had built it up because it was after the incident with Vinny Jones. We played them in a Cup game and beat them 1-0 at our place. It was billed as the Ratcliffe and Jones refight type of thing. It had us side by side in the papers with height, reach, weight and it was ridiculous. It was because of the head butt incident which he denied – he'd also made a bad tackle on Sharpy. I took stick for supposedly taking a dive! He was upset, I think it cost him a boot deal, but if he hadn't put his head near me, he would not have been in that situation. In the game I'd just come back from injury and had my best game for a long time. We won and I think they were the Cup holders at the time. Vinny was sub and when he came on he got the biggest boo you've ever heard. He ran on past Sheeds who thought he was going to chin him. Sheeds had his fists up! It was a game we knew we couldn't lose, live on TV, so they couldn't go round smashing everyone up, and on an even keel we knew no one could come near us!

BK: How did you get on with Gordon Lee?

KR: I thought he was in a different class, to be fair. Many fans didn't like him but he gave me my chance. He was different, he never realised that he was so funny. The lads would just crack up laughing at him and he didn't realise what he'd done. He also had a knack, or an art, you could say, of distracting you and making you lose track of what you'd come to talk to him about. I got dropped once after a game against

Spurs, we played West Brom in the week and I wasn't even in the squad. I marched in to see him, I was was furious over a few things. He's sat at his desk rocking back on his chair. Then he rocked back too far and cracked his head on the cupboard. I couldn't say a thing, I just wanted to get outside and laugh me bollocks off. It was so funny to see the manager like that. Gordon's downfall was when Steve Burtenshaw left at a time when a number of players were at the end of their careers and he got the sack.

BK: What was the story behind the head butt on Tommy Hutchinson?

KR: Didn't like him!! No, I was young, we'd had a bit of a ding dong throughout the game. I wasn't too happy with him and I regretted it and never did it again. It may have cost us a semi-final place. It was one of those things that if you could turn back the clock ...

BK: Who did you rate amongst all the great players around the mid-80s?

KR: Everyone had a different talent in them. Eighty per cent of the goals came from Kevin Sheedy; Trevor was very skilful; Nev was probably the best keeper in the world at the time, and with Reidy, Sharpy, Andy and Inchy, it was just such a good mixture, but the biggest thing about it was that we were nasty!! We were a nasty bunch who wanted to win every game. We had a big togetherness, a team spirit like I've never come across before or since. Now you just see a few on the bench, we had about ten. It was our trademark. When you scored, everyone on the bench was up dancing. Those lads weren't playing, but they were made to feel one of the team. We never treated anyone any differently, the lads on the bench were just as important. Your Kevin Richardsons and Alan Harpers, whoever it was, they were made to feel part of the team.

BK: Why didn't you get a perm when most of the others did?

KR: I had a bushy moustache instead, but I never had a perm. Nor did I have leather pants either, unlike Sharpy! He also had a bad perm along with Inchy and Kevin Richardson. But the funniest sight was Sheeds turning up for pre-season training with blond hair!

BK: Are you aware that you were caught on camera having a piss in the tunnel before the '86 Cup Final?

KR: I always peed in the tunnel before I went out, everywhere. It was my thing, even at Goodison.

BK: Why did you never kick Ian Rush all over the park?

KR: Couldn't get near him! He was an excellent player, a year younger than me and I'd known him since I was fifteen. We became pally with Wales. We had banter and respect. I did kick him and, believe me, I did my best to stop him.

BK: How much did that team socialise together?

KR: During Howard's first reign we all went for a drink after the game. It would only be a couple, then you could drive home. In the Bulldog, or the Sefton. Even Reidy came and he lived in Bolton then. We all went out together and that built the team spirit.

BK: The three goals you scored in your career, what do you remember?

KR: Right foot, left foot and a header. Norwich the right foot, left foot against the Shite, and the header was at Cardiff. I think I scored one in every one hundred and fifty League games, it could have been better but I wasn't allowed up, even though I thought I was the best attacker of the ball at the Club! I could also hang in the air like Sharpy. Mine was more of a spring though. I felt I should have scored more, but with my pace, Howard wanted me at the back. I made a mistake once at QPR and it was never forgotten. I blamed Gary Stevens, he blamed me, and Sheeds just laughed his socks off!

BK: THE best player you played with?

100

KR: They were all great in that side, but if I had to pick one it would have to be the one who was world class – Big Nev. He was outstanding – awesome was the word – he made some fabulous saves and would then say, "I've made better in training," and it was true. Playing out, it was probably Kevin Sheedy – I've not seen a better left foot, his delivery was unbelievable. You have to play with these lads to know how good they are. Peter Reid had amazing determination and that was from somebody who, when he came to the Club, was not even supposed to be playing football because of injury. and the side cost next to nothing!

BK: Best player you've played against?

KR: Here, Rushy, or Dalglish, but then there's Buttragueno, Carreca, Klinnsman, Voller, Sanchez – you can't name just one, it would be unfair on the others.

BK: Hardest player you've played with, or against?

KR: What do you mean by hard? If you mean like Dave Watson, never moaned – he was only hurt if he was knocked out. Reidy was hard and Andy Gray must have been one helluva player at twenty years of age, because when he came to us he was supposedly finished and he was still outstanding, very brave. I think he was trained as a kamikaze pilot who thought he couldn't be killed! He won Young Player of the Year, so you know he must have been some player, and I wouldn't have liked to mark him. There are three players who you would want week in and week out. There's hard and dirty – Jimmy Case was a hard nut – well respected and a good footballer. Souness was hard as well. I know I keep picking them, but they were a good side, but somebody had to take over their mantle and we did it! Then there was John Fashanu – he never caught me but I remember having to pick up Dave Watson once – thank God it wasn't me! The two hardest were Mick Harford and Billy Whitehurst. Billy was an absolute monster. Me and Reidy both went in on him once together and we came off worst! He was the one who finished Brace, more or less, he was certainly one you didn't mess with.

BK: Did anyone ever try and get revenge on Brian Marwood for doing Inchy?

KR: Brian was a good player, I don't think he actually meant it, it was just one of those things. He wasn't a dirty player, I've seen worse tackles where no one was hurt. Unfortunately, it put him out for twelve months and he had only just won the fans over and that had taken a while. Brian regretted it, but it was just one of those things.

BK: Is Gary Lineker on your Christmas Card list?

KR: I've nothing against Gary Lineker. I made him what he is – a TV star! Everton was his kick start but we never won anything with him. After he left we went and won the League again. He was a great player though; one of the best centre forwards I've played with. I had good contact with him, knew where he wanted the ball, but he made his name with us and went on to make his money elsewhere. A good bit of business though, £800k in and £2million out, I think it was, money talks sometimes.

BK: You were in a Wales side with some great players – Big Nev, Hughesy, Rushy and Giggsy. Why weren't they more successful?

KR: Wales could never get a full set of Premier players in their team. We had Second Division players in the side – Mark Bowen, Paul Bodin, Mark Aizlewood – and my last game for Wales I was playing in the Third Division! The step up is massive, people forget. Those players were excellent and never let us down.

BK: What do you put it down to that the great side never managed to beat Man U and clinch what some might call a treble but most definitely would have been the double?

KR: The games were too close, the lads were a bit jaded and the sending off gave them the extra edge. There was a strange atmosphere, a lot of hatred in the ground, and when you get those vibes as a player it's not nice to play in. Anyone who was there knows what I mean.

BK: How did you feel about being robbed of the chance to take on Europe with that great side?

KR: There's no doubt that Heysel broke that side up and cost Everton ruling Europe and the First Division for many a year. Gary, Trevor and Reidy all went. Sharpy was sold. I got a bad injury. Howard went, and within three years the team had gone.

BK: Do you blame Terry Darracott for your bad injury at Sheff Wed in that he could have brought you off earlier?

KR: No, it was my decision and I played on until half-time. It was a funny sensation, I'd never experienced an injury where something pops, then goes back in. I said I felt okay and played on the left wing. It was a hernia they couldn't detect. I was passed between physios and it wasn't until I went to Lilleshall that it was found. Then I came back too quick in a game against Spurs which Gazza played in.

BK: What was the problem with Dai Davies' testicles?

KR: There wasn't a problem – people just said he had no bollocks!

BK: The next question is a long one. Kevin Ratcliffe is a hard man, The Rat is a man's man. The Rat is a man who men want to be and women want to be with. What I want to know is does he have a feminine side? Has he ever sent a beautiful woman flowers? Has he ever stifled a fart on his first date? More to the point, has he ever worn women's underwear?!

KR: I send me wife flowers. I've also sent them to me Mum and the Mother-in-law. Make sure you get this right – I have never worn ladies' underwear, but I have to be honest, I've never managed to stifle a fart.

Just then Kevin proved the point with a humdinger that had Sausage and Kipper gagging! It was time to leave.

STRAIGHT BACK AT YER

PLAYERS, OFFICIALS, STEWARDS and the police bear the brunt of the majority of shouts. Every now and then it's nice to hear them hit back ... and sometimes the fans join in ...

SITTING IN THE PARK END next to the Southampton fans during a very quiet period in the game, the crowd is virtually silent when a goofy lookin' pisshead stands up on his own, turns to the away fans and shouts at the top of his voice, "You lot should be fuckin' ashamed of yourselves, you ruined Di Caprio's career." Stunned silence ... WHAT?

"He went down on that stupid fuckin' boat you lot built!" As the whole crowd burst into uproar a female steward with peroxide streaks approached and told him to sit down. "Fuck off, you! Come back once you've dyed the rest of yer hair." Again the whole crowd was in bulk. As she skulked off a big copper appeared brandishing his truncheon. As he approached the cheeky wag shouts to him, "And you can fuck off an' all." The officer walked straight up to him and reached into his pockets for what we all feared were his handcuffs, but instead he produced a yellow card and held it aloft, Pierluigi Collina style. It was pure pantomime. Well played the copper, both sets of fans were in stitches. **Steve Mc (03/04/03)**

AT THE DIRE SOUTHAMPTON BORE DRAW, Kevin Kilbane was warming up down by the Park End when my mate shouted to Kevin, "Where you going on your holidays next summer, Kev? Bet it won't be to Portugal." Kevin turned around and said, "Nahh, I'm going to Rhyl for the week." Family Enclosure fell about laughing. **Bluethruanthru (22/10/03)**

THIS WAS BACK IN THE LATE SIXTIES in the Paddock. The ref makes a stupid decision, someone in the crowd shouts out, "You soft twat, ref, I could do better if I was blind." A copper (walking past on patrol around the edge of the pitch), shouts back, "That can be arranged." Oh happy days … **Mark (09/12/02)**

AT LONG LAST my good friend Bill finally gets his just rewards with a shout from, of all people, a linesman, sorry – referee's assistant. Seeing the linesman scratching the top of his leg just inside his shorts Bill shouts out, "Are you getting some sort of sexual pleasure out of that, linesman?" Instantly the linesman retorts, "No! Are you?" After terrorising these unsung nonentities for years it was well worth the wait to watch Bill collapse in a heap of laughter with the linesman being applauded from all those fortunate enough to be within earshot. **Gwladys (05/10/03)**

IN THE QUEUE outside the Kop in 1984 for the 'Graeme Sharp' derby, some wag tells a policewoman, "Hey, love, your horse looks knackered." To which she replied, "You would be too, if you'd been between my legs for three hours." The day just got better and better after that. **Mick Upfield (31/10/02)**

I WAS AT THE BOLTON GAME and we were 3-1 up. After we scored the third and were pretty certain of winning, the young kid in front of me began taunting the Bolton players. As we were so close to the pitch they could hear every word he was saying. Warhurst got the worst stick with shouts such as, "Warhurst, your bobble's fell out." The ball came over by us for a Bolton throw and Warhurst came to take it. The kid suddenly screamed, "Hey! Warhurst, get a haircut." To which Warhurst turned around and shouted, "NO," and then flicked his hair as he turned to take the throw. Classic. The kid didn't open his gob for the remainder of the game. **Norman Brown (17/05/02)**

A GOOD FEW YEARS AGO, I think 1996ish, Wimbledon at home. A fella in the Lower Gwladys was heckling Neil Sullivan in their goal all the way through the first half. With the ball at the other end, and the crowd quiet – he stands up and shouts, "Sullivan, I've shagged your wife!" To which Sullivan promptly turns round and shouts back, "I'm not married," with a big smile on his face. He duly received a standing ovation and wiped the smile off the fella's face who never opened his mouth for the rest of the game. **John Coyne (03/04/03)**

THE LAST TIME CHARLTON GOT RELEGATED they played at Everton towards the end of the season. All of Goodison were singing, "Goin' down, goin' down, goin' down," to which the Charlton fans started singing, "So are we, so are we, so are we." Had to laugh. Twats! **Hez (21/05/02)**

WE WERE HAMMERING WEST HAM 5-0 a couple of seasons ago and they were chanting along with us, "We want six, we want six," and when we finally got six they started cheering like mad. A quality day. **Kate's lover (18/12/01)**

AT THE WEST HAM GAME in 1987, Goodison Road Paddock some bloke shouts at the linesman (who was a bit twitchy on the offsides), "Stick that fuckin' flag up your arse, you soft twat." To everyone's amazement the liner turned and shouted in the general direction of the shout, "If I had an arse like yours I would." **Steve Enty (05/10/01)**

IN THE RECENT FA CUP 3RD ROUND MATCH at Plymouth their fans were being very vocal in their support in the first ten minutes. They started singing, "We can't hear you over there" to the Evertonians, to which the lad sat next to me stood up and shouted, "It's 'cos yous lot are making too much fuckin' noise!" Hilarious. Keep up the good work. **Anthony Landau (27/01/05)**

DON'T TAKE US ON!

THEY HAVE ALL TRIED and inevitably failed. So why do other clubs' supporters keep trying to out-smart us?

IPSWICH IN THE SEVENTIES at Portman Road when they had a decent side. We got stuffed 5 something and I was going through all the usual crap – won't be watching Match of the Day, cancel all the newspapers etc. But the gloom was pierced by the joy of being with the incredible Everton away support. Their supporters were desperately trying to take the piss about thieving bastards, scallies and broke into a chorus of, "On the dole! On the dole." Quick as a flash, to the tune of 'Guantanamera', about a thousand Blues started holding their scarves in the air and singing, "One job between us. There's only one job between us." It was picked up by every Evertonian and stunned their supporters into silence. You could hear them thinking, "Er ... we don't do self mockery. You can't take the piss out of yerself, can yer?" You can if you've got style. A wonderful moment. Made me proud to be an Evertonian. **Tony Burke (22/09/03)**

THE CHELSEA HORDES were in full piss-take mode, the score being 2-0 at the time and Radz just having missed a sitter. "Gone to the races, you shoulda gone to the races," they chirped hilariously. Just in front of me a beauty with long flowing locks and nice arse stood up and screeched back, "And yous fuckers shoulda been killed at birth." It was luv at first shriek. **Mark Murphy (13/04/02)**

IN THE NORWICH CUP GAME recently, the Norwich fans were singing really loud all the way through the first half and some guy behind me in the Park End says, "Shut up, you fuckin' yokels, take yer hands of yer sister's legs." **Daytripper (16/01/04)**

EVERTON v LEICESTER CITY, Saturday 20 December 03. There was a little lull in the match and the City supporters started singing out, "Rooney for Chelsea." We in the Park End were not amused. After they died down, a fella behind me perked up with "Heskey for Leicester." A good laugh was had. **Gatenby (04/01/04)**

DURING THE CARLING CUP GAME against Stockport, the Stockport fans madly started chanting, "Who are yer?" to the Evertonians in the Park End. Once it had died down some fella behind us stood up and shouted back, "I'm Ste, and I'm an alcoholic." The look on the Stockport fans' faces was great. **Marko18 (05/10/03)**

JUST AS GRAVESEN was about to take the corner for Super Kev to knock the winner against Boro (14/09), I was sat in the Park End by the Boro gypsies. When all 500 (approx) of them started shouting, "You fat bastard," to a rather chubby looking bloke a few rows back, who was eating what looked like one of many pies. As Kev headed the winner the chunky bloke started shouting, "I'm a fat bastard," to which there was no reply from the gypsies. **Gary (22/09/02)**

WEDNESDAY NIGHT AGAINST BIRMINGHAM, their fans singing, "There's only one Robbie Savage," and some fella in the Lower Gwladys stands up and shouts, "Thank fuck there's no more." Classic. **Philip Lee (10/09/02)**

YEARS AGO NOW, when Charlton played at Wimbledon's ground. Every away game it was the usual chant coming from the home supporters, "You've got one job between yers." But as quick as a flash we replied, "You've got one ground between yers." And they all sat down and shut up. **Martin Christian (05/08/02)**

SAT AT THE ARSE GAME and the Arse fan's are singing, "Vieira wooooo," and Cockney Dan stands up and sings, "Scott Gemmill wooooo." It was funny as fuck. **Ste Enty (17/05/02)**

AT THE WEST BROM GAME this season the West Brom fans originally taunted the Park End with, "Shall we sing a song for you?" Some bloke in front of us came back with, "As long as it's not one by bloody Slade." Classic. **Legend (02/12/02)**

WENT TO THE PLYMOUTH GAME and behind me there was a very quick-witted man. The Plymouth fans were singing, "Shall we sing a song for you?" all game, and he eventually stood up and shouted "It's not a kareoke!" They carried on singing it, so he stood up and bellowed out a Diana Ross. **Peter Jones (27/01/05)**

KEVIN SHEEDY EXCLUSIVE INTERVIEW

ON THURSDAY 25 JULY 2002, Blue Kipper met up with Everton legend Kevin Sheedy and put your questions to him. Kevin, who had one of the best, if not the best, left foot in Everton history, was in fine form and it was both an honour and a privilege to ask the questions on your behalf. Here's what he said.

BK: How did your move from the Redshite to Everton come about?

KS: It was from the Hereford Boys Club, on to Hereford where I served my apprenticeship for a year, signed professional when I was seventeen, but broke into the first team when I was sixteen. Played fifty-four games for Hereford and attracted Liverpool, who made a bid for me after I was spotted by Geoff Twentyman. I remember travelling up there, I didn't really want to sign for them as they had a policy of playing you in the reserves. I wanted to get into the first team straightaway! I was in digs in Anfield so I used to go and watch Everton when I wasn't playing. I saw the young players coming through, people like Adrian Heath, Kevin Ratcliffe and Kevin Richardson, I just made it known through the local paper that I wanted to move, my contract was up and this alerted Everton. I got a call from Howard Kendall towards the end of my contract, shall we say, to see if I was interested in joining Everton and knowing the potential there, I jumped at the chance. Liverpool wanted me to go to Blackpool, certainly not Derby or Everton (who were both interested). They wanted to dictate where you went to so that the move would not benefit a rival. I dug my heels in, waited for my contract to run out, then made my choice. Howard didn't need to sell it to me, I'd been to the games, tasted the atmosphere and knew it was a massive club and it was on the doorstep. I knew Everton were the team for me! It was important for me to make an early impact to rid any of the, 'If he's not good enough for them why should he be good enough for us?' type of comments. My debut was against Watford away and was not very memorable at all. We got beaten 2-0, our next game we beat Villa 5-0 and then I scored at home to Spurs in a 3-1 win and the crowd took to me. Any doubts had been wiped away.

BK: Who was the toughest player you played with and against?

KS: Kevin Ratcliffe, Peter Reid, probably Kevin Ratcliffe. I remember one time a striker had got him off the ball and Kevin had a word with me and told me the next time I got the ball to pass it short to him so he had a fifty/fifty with this same bloke. Sure enough, Kevin got his retribution! Both of them were hard and fair. Against it would be Souness, I nutmegged him once in training and he just laughed. A few years later I nutmegged him in the Milk Cup Final and he elbowed me in the face. I suppose that's the difference when you're playing for real.

BK: What was the background to you leaving Everton and how did you feel?

KS: (Big gulp), it's difficult to say really. Shall we say some managers fancy you and some don't. Howard was a big fan of mine but when Colin took over, we really didn't hit it off. My career started to slide away when Colin took over, I was in and out of the team and it was not what I wanted. We had a few fall outs and I was looking to get away. Howard came back and things improved for a short while but the team was breaking up. The opportunity came to move to Newcastle under Kevin Keegan. I have never been money orientated so moving after nine years and eight months was what I wanted at the time, I didn't even think twice about a testimonial, I wanted first team football. It turned out a good move as I won another Championship medal and you can't put a price on those things. After that I moved to Blackpool, which wasn't the best of moves but it did give me first team football, it let me down gently from top flight football, so there was a plus to going there. And, no, I didn't visit Owen Oyston on the inside, visiting him on the outside was bad enough!

BK: Who was the best player you played alongside at Everton?

KS: It is difficult to pick a player out of that great Everton side. If I had to pick one it would be Kevin Ratcliffe because he enabled us to play the way we did because of his pace at the back. We could squeeze right up to the half-way line, any balls that came over the top into our defence, then Kevin just went into overdrive and mopped everything up. Adrian Heath and Graeme Sharp were the best striking partnership I have ever played with. Whenever I was on the ball I had an understanding with those two as to exactly where they would be and where they wanted the ball, compared to someone like Tony Cottee, who you didn't know where he was going to run or where he wanted the ball!

BK: What was your best goal for Everton and why do you choose that goal?

KS: There are a few that spring to mind, the one against the Shite, the Ipswich free-kick, the semi-final equaliser against Luton, but if I had to pick one it would be Rapid Vienna. To score in a European final is special and it was the goal that killed the game. We knew we'd won when that one went in.

BK: How did it feel when you planted the second Ipswich free-kick into the net after the ref had disallowed the original beauty?

KS: Reidy was stood over the ball and I told him I still fancied it, I think after putting the first one in that Paul Cooper had over-compensated to stop me doing the same again. It was a good feeling.

BK: When you stepped up to take the free kick v Luton at Villa Park – did you mean to hit it low? Because just about every fan in the ground was expecting the opposite?

KS: I'm not going to say no, am I? Of course I meant to hit it low, I didn't catch it cleanly but it went in. I looked at the wall and how they'd lined up, I saw the gap and went for it. I didn't hit it particularly well but it went in and that was all that mattered. We hadn't played well that day but we had clawed our way back and when it went in it gave us the impetus to go on and win. Deadly Derek did the rest. I always knew where Derek would be and he went on to put it in and win it for us.

BK: Then what was it like to have a large number of bobble-hatted screaming fans bearing down on you when the ball had hit the back of the net?

KS: I didn't really notice, as I was ecstatic with my own celebrations. I was mobbed by players and fans it was a great feeling.

BK: What was it like scoring in a Euro final?

KS: As I said, it was probably the best goal I scored for Everton because of the timing. It meant we'd won the game, you could tell that from the reaction of the players and fans.

BK: Why, when you scored in that Derby game against them from across the park, in one of those silly Super Cup games, with one of your trademark free kicks, did you give the Kop the two-fingered salute. I thought it was class and I still do. Why did you do it?

KS: It was just the way I felt at the time, it was a great free kick and being at the Kop end it just seemed the thing to do. It got me into trouble though.

BK: Do you think heading the ball is over-rated?

KS: It wasn't one of my strengths! Kevin Ratcliffe used to say to me, "You can't tackle, you can't head the ball and you haven't got a right foot!" I used to say to him, "Once you've lost your pace, you'll be finished!" I can't show you my stitches from my headed goal against Man U as they are in my hair, so I can't even prove it to you! Even with that goal, people said Kevin Moran had headed the back of my head to give it the power to go in!

BK: Who was your best pal at Goodison?

KS: I always shared a room and was best friends with Kevin Ratcliffe.

BK: How often do you see other members of the 1985 squad and when, if ever, did you last all get together?

KS: We meet up now and again but I don't think we've ever had the full squad together because there are so many different commitments. It would be nice if we were all back together sometime but probably unrealistic.

BK: Give us the insight into your ruck with Keown?

KS: Next question …

BK: What happened on that 'Chinese bonding' meeting in Southport?

KS: Next question …

BK: How ugly is Martin Keown?

KS: Keown was VERY ugly!

BK: How hard was Psycho Pat?

KS: He was a good player, but put it this way, if there was a fifty/fifty tackle involving Kevin Ratcliffe and Pat Van Den Hauwe I'd back Kevin every time

BK: Why didn't you make more out of the tackle by Phil Neale in the '84 Milk Cup Final? That tackle ended your season and cost you a place in the FA Cup Final in '84. This is a thing that gets my blood pressure going. The England right back that was the perfect gent, who went in studs up and went down

116

your leg, when you were giving him a hard time. He took a vital cog out of Everton's side that day.

KS: Good question, it was a bad tackle by Phil. At the time I didn't realise how bad it was. I had a shot at goal and normally I'd have expected to score from there but it was a really weak shot. That night in bed my wife accidentally kicked my leg and I nearly went through the roof. It was disappointing I missed the FA Cup, and that one tackle did cost me a medal.

BK: What were the saddest and happiest moments in your Everton career?

KS: The saddest moment was leaving Everton. I left under a cloud after a great career, there were many happy moments, just loads of them, obviously the special night – Bayern Munich, winning the Leagues and the Cups, probably Rotterdam was the happiest moment because it meant so much to win a European trophy. It's just a pity we were denied the opportunity to go on and do more.

BK: Why was the left peg SO good?

KS: I practised day in and day out against the back wall of my parents' pub, oh, and I had to pay for a few broken windows!

BK: Can you remember the first time Everton were awarded a freekick and the crowd growled, "SHEEDY"?

KS: Not really, but it was special to hear the fans. I can remember the fans shouting my name when we got a free kick, and I was in the stands having left Everton. That was special.

BK: How were your feelings knowing you had been robbed of something extremely special? (Do you feel the same way as the fans?)

KS: The chance to play in Europe against the best was undoubtedly robbed from us, we all felt that way but there was nothing we could do about it. There's no doubt it caused the break-up of the team!

BK: What moment made you most proud to be wearing an Everton shirt?

KS: The very first time I pulled the shirt on and ran out. The hairs stand up on the back of you neck. There were many other memorable occasions, as you can imagine, particularly the European Final.

BK: Did I fall asleep and miss something – a living Everton legend – did you get a testimonial?

KS: I think I answered that earlier, I've never been money orientated, the money wasn't important to me, I wanted to play first team football and that was all there was to it, even though I was only a few months short of the testimonial I just wanted to play and, if you like, Everton didn't fancy me, so off I went.

BK: Are you and Waggy going to come home one day?

KS: I'd like to, but I don't know about Waggy.

BK: Any chance of returning to Goodison one day in a coaching capacity?

KS: I'd love to, but who knows what will happen in the future?

BK: Any tales from Bellefield, there must have been a few pranks?

KS: One classic was about Andy Hinchcliffe. He prided himself on owning horses. One weekend they were rustled! Andy came in on the Monday and explained he'd be late on the Tuesday because he had to see the police first thing. He ran on to the training ground about 10.30am and was furious. Kevin Ratcliffe had brought a catering size tin of dog food in and left it under the hook in his changing place!

BK: Did you ever go for a pint with Paul McGrath?

KS: I can't remember!

BK: Why Ireland and not Wales? I still can't get my head around that. Wales late mid to late 80s could have done with you and I'm sure would have qualified for a major event.

KS: Basically Wales did not want me, or it felt that way. Ireland
        contacted me and asked me to play, I was only nineteen so I
        phoned Wales and asked if they wanted me to play for them.
        They said they would look into it. They didn't sound too keen
        and never got back to me. So in the end it was an easy
        decision as it was made for me.

BK: Which felt better, the goal against Rapid Vienna, or the goal
        against England in World Cup '90?

KS: The Rapid Vienna goal was very very special from a personal
        point of view as it secured the win and the trophy but from an
        individual point of view the goal against England was very
        special too, as it helped us get to the quarter finals. Overall, I
        would have to pick the goal for Ireland, because as a boy you
        dream of scoring for your country on the biggest stage
        possible – the World Cup.

BK: What do you think Everton need to do to be able to attract
        quality players to the Club once again?

KS: It starts with success, I believe that David Moyes has it in him
        to make Everton successful again, it will take a few years but
        with financial backing, we can do it.

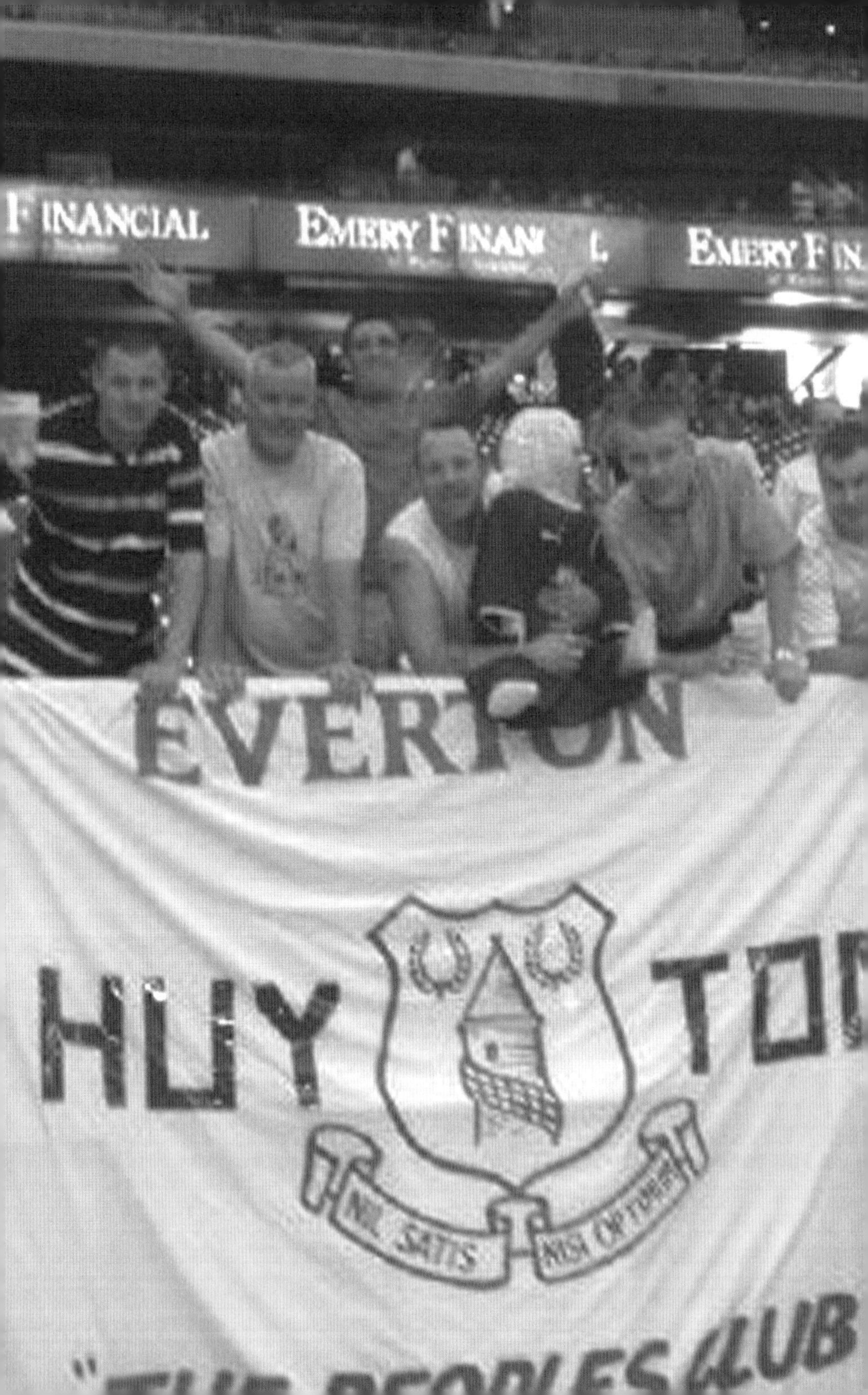
FINANCIAL
EMERY F
EMERY F
HUY
NIL SATIS
NISI OPTIMUM
CLUB

AWAY DAY FUNNIES

THERE IS SOMETHING SPECIAL about trips away with the Toffeemen ...

IT'S OFTEN THE CASE that these stories, when related outside of the prevailing atmosphere, fall flat, and are awarded the epitaph, "... Er, well. It sounded funny at the time, anyway." One such occasion was 10 March 1984 when we played Notts County in the FA Cup quarter final, the one when Andy Gray nearly broke his nose heading in a free kick on the floor. There had been a torrential downpour prior to the match, and I had a ticket at the opposite end of the ground to my mates, and was concerned as to whether we would be able to see the match together. I needn't have worried. When we got there, everyone was just bunking in, and coppers were just watching them, so the ground was over-capacity, and 'specs' were at a premium. In the opening moments, one spaced-out knobhead decided to secure a better vantage point by scaling the floodlight pylon. Response from the crowd varied from concern to anger at their view being obstructed. Then, suddenly, Kevin Richardson scored after 5 minutes, and the mood changed. By this time, the dickhead had climbed about 50 feet to an array of ribald comments, general stick and some good old-fashioned moaning. When it died down, one dry wit drawled out, "Fuckin' 'ell ... an' all because the lady loves Milk Tray." It was funny at the time, and the ensuing laughter nearly caused him to fall off. **Janet and Gerry (12/09/04)**

LAD IN FRONT OF ME at Leeds when Kewell came down to take a corner, "Eh! Harry! Yer bird is gettin' shagged by a Dingle." Second best moment of the day. **Si (11/11/02)**

1989 FA CUP away to Barnsley. Everton were winning 1-0, when Barnsley had a controversial offside given against them. This lad behind me and me arl feller shouts, in a broad Yorkshire accent, "Ey up, linesman, you fucking useless, bald-headed, bandy-legged bastard, stick that fucking flag up your arse, you wanker." On hearing this, me arl feller turns to me and says, "I see the reporter from The Times is here, then." Everyone around us fell about laughing. **Andrew Lee (04/01/03)**

LAST SEASON on the way out of Filbert Street after another disappointing away performance. A female steward, with short dark hair and round glasses, smiles as hundreds of Blues pile out of the away end. Some Blue starts the chant, "One Harry Potter, there's only one Harry Potter," quickly followed by hundreds of Blue voices, "ONE HARRY POTTER ..." etc. The only piece of entertainment any Bluebelly got all afternoon. **The Mexican Bank Robber (11/11/02)**

AWAY TO SHEFF WED, a few seasons ago. Queueing up outside when one Evertonian shouts to a policewoman on a horse "Eh, love, what time do you get off?" to which the policewoman replies "None of your business." Everton fan replies, "Wasn't talking to you, love, I was talking to the horse." **Joe Cody (05/08/02)**

AT LEEDS GAME A couple years ago, when Bowyer and Woodgate were in court. Bowyer takes a corner and some fella in front stands up and shouts, "At least you don't have to worry 'bout droppin' the soap in the shower, you're a fuckin' ugly twat." **Blue 4 eva BW (04/11/02)**

AT THE PRESTON friendly last week when over at the dugout Scot Gemmill and Mark Pembridge were warming up. All of a sudden the man behind shouts, "Fuckin' hell, Moyes, I bet they're quaking in their boots now, eh?" **Alan (22/08/03)**

FRIENDLY AGAINST CREWE when Rhino was just about to take a throw-in and some lad yells, "Go 'ed, Slim!" Even Unsey chuckled to himself! **Creevy (15/08/03)**

I WAS AT THE LEICESTER GAME at Filbert Street a few years back in the Leicester End. A Leicester player went down injured just as a Foxes fan stood up to go to the bog. The fan turned around and asked who it was. Another fan said, "It's Heskey." To which he replied, "Oh, good, I've got time for a shit then." **John Harris (15/08/03)**

WHEN OUR COACH ARRIVED at the Stadium of Light the nice local constabulary got on the coach to read their riot act as to what we could or could not do at the ground. At the end of the Gestapo-like speech he asked the coach party "Any questions?" to which Marti shouted, "What's the capital of Peru?" The coach fell about laughing. Even the plod's face had a little smirk on it, or it could have been wind ... **Ian MacDonald (24/12/01)**

LAST SEASON away at Boro, with my mates, Pete, Pete Snr and Jonathan. Uriah Rennie wasn't givin' many decisions our way and the fat fella behind us shouts, "Fuck of, Uriah! You're givin' me indigestion!" **Ste Willetts (22/07/03)**

A FEW SEASONS BACK we beat West Ham 4-0 away. The ref, Paul Alcock, was having an absolute shocker as usual and after about the tenth ridiculous decision, some fat bastard next to me starts singing, "All cock, no brain, all cock no brain, all cock no brain ..." **Ade (22/07/03)**

MIDDLE 80s away at Bradford in the Cup. George Courtney was referee. Young lad screaming all kinds of stuff at him and it all goes quiet except for this one young Toffee going off his nut. He finally takes a breath, realises it's gone quiet and yells out, "Oi! Courtney! Yer missus has got two arse-holes ... You're one of 'em." Even Courtney had a smile on his face. **Kris Everton (yes it really is my name, I changed it by deed poll) (17/11/03)**

CHELSEA AWAY and Amokachi is warming up by us and some Chelsea stiff jogs by behind him. My brother shouts, "Oi! Ammo! That bloke behind you just called you a twat!" Ammo turned round and the Chelsea sub put his hands up and went, "No I never." **The BlueClown (24/10/02)**

SHREWSBURY had a very attractive looking (female) physio who was treating one of their attackers at the far end from the visiting Blues behind the goal, when one of the lads shouted to the Shrewsbury goalie in front of us, "Go down, keeper." **BarlickBlue (27/07/02)**

AWAY TO SOUTHAMPTON about ten or twelve years ago, Southall is giving the back four a piece of his mind, effing and blinding. You know what it's like at The Dell, you can hear everything. At half-time, as Nev goes to get his bag out of the goal, a copper comes over and starts bollocking him for his language saying that there's been complaints from people with children. He's talking to Nev like he's a little kid, so this wag shouts out, "Hey! Nev! Tell him to fuck off." **John Black (09/07/02)**

AT HIGHBURY, last game of this season. Arsenal were showing the trophy to the Everton fans, who were giving them a good rally. By the way, Jeffers was right at the back of the group of Arsenal players. Anyway, Tony Adams and Martin Keown brought the trophy really close to the fans. We were a couple of rows from the front. This fella just behind screamed at the top of his voice, "Martin, Martin, Martin." Keown looked at this fella. The Fella shouts, "Martin! Any regrets at leaving Everton?" The whole place was in stitches. Keown, with the Premiership Trophy in his hands, laughed his head off. **Ged (21/05/02)**

AT AN OXFORD AWAY GAME in Feb 1987, we were all squeezed into the cesspit of the Cuckoo Lane away end and the lads were losing 1-0. The permed Paul Wilkinson is standing hopefully in the penalty box up our end awaiting a cross and with his arms aloft waving. One very loud wag behind shouts out, "For Christ's sake, Blues, don't pass to the fucking hairdresser." Amazingly, the hirsute Wilko had the last laugh with an injury-time equaliser. **Doug, Kent Blue (26/11/01)**

MY BROTHER AND I were at the famous 'lowest ever Premiership crowd' game at Wimbledon, a freezing wet Tuesday night in January at Selhurst Park, 1992/93, I think. The official attendance was 3,033, which seemed to consist of 3,000 Evertonians packed into one section and 33 Wimbledon fans. First hint of the small crowd was when I parked the car 5 yards from the gate. Neville had to go and get the ball back when the first shot went over the bar, they eventually sent some poor kid to sit on the terrace to get the ball back. The ball goes out right in front of the Everton fans and a Wimbledon player with number 39 on his back picks it up and goes to take the throw-in. A wag in the front row shouts, "Fuckin' 'ell, lad. If there are thirty-eight Wimbledon players better than you, you must be shite!" You've never seen anyone's shoulders slump so quickly or so low, and he fucked up the throw as well. Crowd was in hysterics, so were some of the players. Worth the trip – we won 3-1. **Blooblud (24/08/04)**

1990 AWAY AT VILLA and we are getting pasted 6-0. An own goal sets us up at 6-1, and the whole away end goes fucking mental like we'd just scored the winner in the Cup Final. Still laughing our heads off, I think Cottee gets us a second and we go mental again. As the cheering subsides we turn to the Villa End and start chanting, "EASY, EASY, EASY!" Crying, I was. **Spart (02/04/02)**

AT MIDDLESBROUGH. Six thousand Evertonians packed into the away section … but loads of empty home seats. The obvious chants of, "Shit ground, no fans, shit ground, no fans," repeatedly. Until a voice pipes up, "But Goodison *is* a dump." Murmurs of agreement and chant changes to, "Nice ground, no fans, nice ground, no fans." Well there wasn't much else to smile about. **PJEFC (22/03/02)**

FINAL WHISTLE AT BORO. The ones of us that still remained were leaving our seats. Getting loads of grief from the Boro fans just yards away. Usual tanked-up Blues shoutin' back, "fuck off, twats ... Boro are shite ... you bunch of wankers ... etc." Then over the tannoy, "Next up at the Riverside, next Saturday ... Boro versus the shite." The loudest Blue, who has been shoutin' the most abuse, immediately shouts out, "Come on, Boro." It nearly made us laugh anyway. **PJEFC. (18/03/02)**

THE RECENT TRIP TO PORTSMOUTH, standing there in the pissin' down rain when the Pompey fans started singing, "Stand up if you love Pompey." Fella at the back of us starts singing, "Stand up if your seats are wet." Had us all in stitches. **Tom Bell. (20/12/03)**

WHEN YOU'RE SMILING ...

OVER THE SEASON Evertonians have developed the ability to keep ourselves entertained, even if the action on the pitch is nothing to smile about ...

I REMEMBER STANDING in the Paddock in the early 70s watching the Blues play WBA. The game was awful and the ref was having a nightmare. One fella shouted, "Who's the fucking ref?," and the reply came from behind. "The one in the black, you soft bastard." **Lynchblueboy (29/09/01)**

3-0 DOWN TO TRANMERE, 92nd minute, loads of Blues leaving and the rest of us sitting in abject misery. My day was brightened by one comedian at the front of the Upper Gwladys standing up and shouting, "Come on ... you're leaving it late Blues." **Stuart Brandwood (29/09/01)**

HEARD AT OUR END at the Charlton game this season. Bloke behind me, "Awwww, that Stubbsy's class, innee?" Bloke behind me, "Fuck off, 'es just like Unzie ... 'cept sexier ..." Pure class. **Declan Clark (26/09/01)**

A FAVOURITE OF MINE is only heard when Pembridge has a shot on goal ... "DUCK!" (I sit in the Upper Gwladys). **Carl Stewart (25/09/01)**

DURING THE 80s, we played Derby County, who Bruce Rioch was managing at the time. The Gwladys Street were shoutin', "Everton reject" to him. A young scally shouted, "Who's the reject?" One of me none-too-sober mates shouted out, "Rioch, son. He was 'ere, when you woz shittin' yella!" **Paul C Clarke (26/09/01)**

AT THE SPURS GAME, after a great through ball from the 'Chinese Beckham' (which The Rad slotted), the crowd around us kicked off with, "There's only one Li Tie, one Li Tie." When it all calmed down some wag shouted, "Is there fuck! There's three hundred and sixty million of them." **Shortalls (27/01/03)**

ABOUT FIVE MINUTES from the end of the Villa match, April 2003. The ball is flicked on by Duncan Ferguson in the direction of 'super' Kevin Campbell. He turns to reach the flick on and falls flat on his arse. A lad about four seats along from me in the upper Gwladys shouts, "Friggin' hell, Campbell. I wish my missus went down as often as you." When the laughter died down it was followed by a shout from a couple of rows behind of, "SHE DOES!" Happy days. **Jimmy (09/05/03)**

I REMEMBER being in the Paddock, early 70s and this bloke shouts, "Darracott! You're shite!" Voice from behind says, "There's no need for inappropriate language." "Sorry mate," came the reply and then, "Darracott, you're fucking shite." **Hughesie (23/09/01)**

AT THE LEICESTER GAME when one of their players was taking his time about limping off the pitch to waste some time as we were still 2-0 down. The little lad in front of me grew increasingly impatient and being only about 7 shouted, "'Urry up, you idiot." Everyone around had a slight laugh at the passion of this young fan, but then the bloke next to him says, "Eh, there's no need for language like that, there's ladies present." I found the blokes sarcasm funny, as did most who sit around me. **Emma (20/04/02)**

HEARD IN THE TOP BALCONY on the Good Friday derby, when short arse Owen lay injured, "Oh dear, the baby Jesus is dead." Reply from two rows back, "Don't worry, he'll be back on Sunday." **Billythebluecat (21/09/01)**

DOES ANYBODY REMEMBER a bloke in the Lower Bullens Paddock who used to constantly sing, "Andy Gray, Andy Gray, Andy Gray ..." seasons after he had left? He also used to make this weird sound like a Red Indian when everything went quiet. You could even hear him on TV when the Blues were on live! **Ian Gilchrist (20/09/01)**

IN RESPONSE to Ian Gilchrist's 'shout' (See above). I remember the bloke he referred to, we knew him as 'the clapper' because he would carry on clapping long and hard after everyone else had stopped. This was long before his adulation of Andy Gray but his Tonto noise was legendary. **Chris Simpson (29/09/01)**

CHELSEA AT HOME, a couple of seasons ago. Blues 2-1 up, after falling behind. Cadamarteri receives the ball out wide, deep in Chelsea's half, with about a minute left. He gets various shouts of, "Hold!" "Get down to the corner flag," and "Play it off him for a throw." Unable to stand the tension any longer, a fella behind me in the Street End bellowed, "Oh fuck it, just run with it, yer daft little bastard!" **Andrew Hill (09/05/03)**

A FEW YEARS AGO, when Norwich gave us a 5-1 stuffing, some fella shouts, "Fuckin' 'ell! Getting stuffed by ten canaries and Ekoku." **Simon Lloyd (20/04/02)**

HALF-TIME AT CHELSEA on Saturday. A fella behind me was discussing the 1st half with his mate and was asked if he thought we should do any substitutes. He said, "I think I would bring on Chadwick ... for Cudicini and Hasselbaink." Class. **Paul Truss (12/04/02)**

GAME AGAINST CREWE and Walter takes off our last remaining Swedish international. Shout: "Fuck me, Walter, you've taken off all the Swedes and left the fucking cabbages on the pitch." **Mark Williams (25/02/02)**

AT THE ORIENT GAME and the chants of, "Gazza for England" are echoing out, some fella behind stands up and shouts, "Unsworth for Slim Fast." Absolute quality. **Tony (16/02/02)**

ONE MATCH in the early 90s, it was mid-week, cold and a crap game (pretty typical of the 90s). It also happened to be the game in which Paul Holmes was making his debut. Anyway, in a particularly poor passage of play one wag in the Lower Gwladys shouts out, "For fuck's sake, we've got a Watson and a Holmes and we still haven't got a fuckin' clue." PRICELESS. **Paul Duckworth (11/02/02)**

ANOTHER CLASSIC from the boxing day debacle against Man Utd, was halfway through the second half, the bloke behind me was becoming impatient at Walter Smith putting Unsworth in midfield. He stood up and screamed, "Hey! Smith! We got no chance with that midfield, look, we got two Swedes and a turnip." Quality. **Neil (21/01/02)**

AT THE CREWE GAME I was getting a pie when some fella in front of me was getting one of them shitty pizzas and the woman behind the counter said, "What are you having, love?" He replied, "Food poisoning by the look of it." **Street End Blue (20/02/02)**

... THE WHOLE WORLD SMILES WITH YOU

AT THE FIRST GAME of the season against Arsenal. We were getting a good hiding, 3-0 down at the time. Some fella shouts, "Bring the elephant on!" referring to the poor fella dressed up as an elephant, promoting Chang Beer. **Cookie (16/08/04)**

CHARLTON GAME, and Gravesen goes steaming forward, only to clatter into Lee Carsley. Usual comedian behind us shouts, "Bet he shit himself, thought he was running into a mirror." **Mike Bennett (18/11/02)**

AT THE LAST HOME GAME of the season v Bolton. The Bolton fans started singing, "You need Rivaldo, you need Rivaldo ..." (to which everyone agreed). Then, when it all went quiet, some fella starts chanting to the tune of 'Who Needs Cantona?', "WHO NEEDS RIVALDO, WHEN WE'VE GOT LEE CARSLEY?" **Chris S (02/07/04)**

WHEN NAYSMITH SCORED the free kick against Spurs, the lad sat next to me said, "I see that he's bought Kevin Sheedy's left foot on Ebay." **Dave Cederholm (04/05/04)**

DURING THE RECENT GAME against Leicester, Marcus Bent was minding his own business when some lout stood up and shouted, "Oi! Marcus! Is that yer name, or a fuckin' statement?" Made me laugh anyway. **James Bates (13/02/04)**

I THINK IT WAS THE 1-4 REVERSAL against Villa a few years back, when some frustrated fan ran on to the pitch. After the fuzz dragged him away, the announcer tells us, "He will be barred from Goodison for his stupidity." Somebody shouts, "Lucky bastard". **Richard Jones (06/02/03)**

LEAVING GOODISON after the Blackburn game, a seriously stressed street seller was surrounded by a massive crowd of supporters all trying to buy his 'Roonaldo' posters. The poor guy couldn't cope – he couldn't roll the posters up quick enough to meet demand and he was fast running out of pockets to stuff his money into. Recalling a somewhat less hectic time he'd had with a previous poster, he said, "Come back, Alan Biley, all is forgiven." **Joe The Bookie (23/12/02)**

AT ONE POINT in the Chelsea match (7 December 2002), when Everton's midfield wasn't quite getting things together, someone near me in the Upper Bullens shouted: "Come on, Gravesen and Li Tie, you're not speaking the same language." **School of Science (15/12/02)**

ABOUT 10 YEARS AGO when Preki (Pedrag Radosavlevic) was playing, some bloke shouts out, "What the fuck does Preki mean?" A joker then stands up and shouts, "It's Yugoslav for shite." Priceless. **Nich (09/12/02)**

THIS HAPPENED AT THE HOME MATCH against Crystal Palace on the opening day of the 1997/98 season. Palace were 1-0 up at half-time against a labouring home side and went further ahead when Bruce Dyer scored a penalty in the second half. Over the PA system, the announcer declared, "The scorer of the second goal for Crystal Palace is Dyer." From a few rows behind me in the Upper Gwladys someone remarked loudly, "With a name like that he should be in our team." **Keith (26/10/02)**

I WAS IN THE MAIN STAND about 10 years ago, I can't remember who we were playing but it was a night match. It was cold, wet, and we were playing terribly. Halfway through the second half, the lights went out leaving the stadium in complete darkness. After a few cheers from the crowd, the lights were soon put back on. As soon as the lights came back on, some bloke shouts, "Turn the fuckin' lights off, I'm trying to have a kip here." In quick reply some other bloke further down shouts, "Hey! fuck off! I've been readin' me book for an hour now." **Phil Jones (18/11/02)**

WAS IN THE TOP BALCONY at the Leeds match and some fella was clearly frustrated with Rhino playing the ball on the ground. Rhino got the ball and this fella shouted, "HOOF IT." Everyone in the Top Balcony keeled over in hysterics. A few nearly fell over the edge. **Hicker (13/10/03)**

AGAINST NEWCASTLE when Tommy Grav was holding the ball for our free kick. Some fella shouts, "Hurry up, yer baldy prick." To which some fella carrying the pies back to his place replies, "I'm coming, I'm coming." **Kate's lover (26/11/01)**

ME AND MY GIRLFRIEND, Laura, were at the Boro game, when this bloke pipes up behind us, "Get the ball up to the big lad up front." To which someone replied, "He's Bent." Then Laura said, "It doesn't bother me, I'd still shag him." Had half the Gladdy in stitches – Classic. **Kenno Gladdy (28/09/04)**

AT THE EVERTON ARSE GAME – 2004. First game of the season with the clouds and naysayers all around us. The Arse were giving the 'School of Science' a lesson in how to play football. Wenger decides to bring Reyes off and bring Pires on. My mate turns around to me and says, "That's just effin' great, they're taking off Batman and they're bringing on Superman." You had to laugh. **John Bracken (28/09/04)**

IT WAS AGAINST ARSENAL, first game of the season, and the Chang elephant walked on to the pitch. Someone in front pipes up, "Fuck off, Unsworth. We sold you in the summer." Our corner of the Gwladys was in stitches. **Leigh Beach (21/09/04)**

WHEN YOBO SCORED his second Everton goal in two games against Spurs, I said to the arl fella in front of me, "He's prolific that Yobo, isn't he?" The arl fella replied, "Nah – he's defo Nigerian." **Robbie G (24/04/04)**

PLAYING CHARLTON AWAY. Dull game. We won 1-0. Mike Newell scored. We played shite though. Sheedy havin' an unusually poor game when some arl fella shouts, "Eh! Sheed! Yer a lazy twat, I'll get the ball for yer," (after Sheedy failed to run on to a pass). Then some arl girl pipes up (and she must've been 60+), "Eh! You! (total silence) Less of your fucking swearing, yer dirty twat." Mass laughter in Everton Away End. **Astro (24/04/04)**

I WAS AT THE BRUM MATCH on Boxing Day, when the Brummie ball boy tried three times to throw or kick the ball over the net back to Richard Wright, and failed miserably. Some genius pipes up with, "Even their ball boys are shit." Class. **Andrew Lee (04/01/03)**

DURING HALF-TIME against Leeds a couple of years ago and Martyn, Bridges and Hart were warming up, when one of their balls flew into the Gwladys Street, never to be returned. Another two soon followed and stayed in the crowd. Next minute the Everton fans were singing, "One ball, you've only got one ball ..." Even Michael Bridges was in stitches. **Paddy (13/11/02)**

AT THE ARSENAL MATCH 2002 at Goodison, when Franny 'The Ears' Jeffers comes on and the crowd chants, "There's only one greedy bastard." The fella behind, who's had about four pies throughout the game and weighed 25 stone+, starts to sing, "There's only two greedy bastards." **Ryan Hand (11/11/02)**

PARK END AGES AGO when we had Ginola. He was warming up with Gravesen on the sideline, talking and laughing. A fella behind me shouts, "Ginola. You know you can't discuss hair products with him. He's fuckin' bald." **Callum (03/09/03)**

THE LEEDS GAME, Robinson taking a goal kick at the Gwladys Street End, some fella shouts, "Hey! Robbo! They've sold your team bus, you've got to fucking walk home." Quality. **Mick H (18/02/03)**

AT THE FULHAM AWAY GAME on Saturday. Kilbane controlled a simple ball and passed it short to the nearest Everton player. The guy behind shouts, "This game's too easy for yer, Zinedine." Made me laugh for ages. **Paul (16/01/04)**

THIS WASN'T AT A MATCH, but last season in the massive 6-hour queue for season tickets, some tit pulls up and asks, "Is this the queue for season tickets?" To which some fella replied, "No, mate, it's the queue for Scott Gemmill's autograph!" Made the whole line chuckle. **Carl McConnell (05/12/03)**

AT THE SOUTHAMPTON GAME this season (shit). When the announcer comes up and says, "Attention! Operation Exercise Goodison is about to commence." Some guy stands up and shouts, "What are we doing? Star jumps?" and he starts doing some star jumps. Very funny. Then when the announcer says, "Operation Exercise Goodison is a success." The same guys start cheering madly, cue many laughs. Highlight of the game. **Howell (25/10/03)**

I WAS MEETING SOMEONE by the Dixie Dean statue. "Hey, was he that big?" "Yeah." "No wonder he scored sixty goals then." **Paul BW (17/11/03)**

READING ALL THESE I am reminded of a couple of corkers. The first was a few seasons back, we were playing Blackburn Rovers, about the time when we had an ageing Limpar and Claus Thomsen in midfield. It had been a dull game, not many shots, and the Blues were shooting into the Gwladys against Tim Flowers. Someone shouts out, "Oi! Tim! D'you fancy a cuppa?" Everyone, including Flowers, pissed themselves. **Paul Barrett (05/08/02)**

MUST'VE BEEN 95/96ish, sitting in our usual spec, Lower Gwladdy, this arl fella who constantly moans sat behind us for a whole season. Anyway, a pacey through ball wasn't met by one of our strikers (dunno, maybe Rideout), this fella pipes up, "He'll never get to that, the fastest thing on the pitch is always the ball," to which the bloke next to him replies, "Well, buy two fuckin' balls an stick 'em up front then." Class. **Al. N. Wales Blue (12/06/02)**

LAST HOME GAME OF THE SEASON against Blackburn, awful game. The highlight is a ginger streaker right at the end. I sit in the Park Stand and a guy two rows behind me shouts "I was wondering where Pembridge was." It was brilliant. **Dave Manchester (03/05/02)**

V CHELSEA AT HOME – in the Lower Bullens – this blonde streaks on to the pitch with nothin' but a red thong on. The granddad behind puts his hands over his grandson's eyes and says, "Red knickers? At Goodison – that's disgraceful." Classic. **Gezza (04/10/01)**

TWO SEASONS AGO, 1999, when we had the midfield trio of Hutch, Judas and Collins. It was Boxing Day, against Derby at home. I was sitting with me Dad after winning tickets on the radio (City FM). I was in the Family Enclosure (Park End in the corner) when we won a corner. Hutch ran over to take it, and a man in front shouted, "Merry Christmas, Don." Hutch turned round and looked but didn't recognise the voice. Anyway, he took the corner and nothing came of it. About 5 minutes later, after Cada had a shot tipped over the bar, Hutch ran over (same side) and put the ball down ... a voice again came out from the crowd (same fella), "... And a happy new year." The fans around him burst out laughing. Hutch turned round with a grin on his face. Class. That was about the best of the action from the game (0-0). **Toffee Man Dan (18/01/02)**

NOT SO MUCH A SHOUT more an observation. Me and my muckers Blue Kev and Blue Mac are standing outside the Spellow enjoying our usual pre-match beverage and chat before the game v Black Cats. Next thing, bloke leaves the bar with nout in the bottom of the pint glass he's carrying. Goes into house opposite (can't disclose number), and two minutes later, hey presto, he's going back into the ale house with a full pint – Quality. **Mark Thomas (15/01/02)**

GOODISON PARK LATE 90s. Nevin has just scored a wonderful goal. Bloke One, "That Pat Nevin's great." Bloke Two, equally enthralled, "Yeah, he likes Jesus and Mary Chain." Classic. **Kevin (01/10/01)**

REDSHITE

AS DIFFICULT AS IT IS to have a whole chapter devoted to them, hate them or hate them, you have to admit they give us plenty to smile about ...

WHEN ME AND A MATE were at Analfield this season in the Kopite End, Everton fans were singing, "And if yer know your history." And some Welsh Redshite bastard turns round and says, "What history? You ain't got none." My mate comes back saying, "What you on about? We won the League on this ground before you existed." Even Kopites were laughing. Classic. **Toffeenose80 (03/06/04)**

ME MATE'S DAD (in his 60s and a life-long Evertonian) was at a sporting celebrity evening dinner in the early 70s with his brother-in-law who is a Red. Present at the dinner was Ian St John. Said brother-in-law did not have the courage to ask the Kopite hero for an autograph, so he persuaded me mate's dad to get one for him. Me mate's dad gave St John a piece of paper and said, "Could you sign this four times please?" The famous Red duly obliged and then asked, "Why did you want me to sign it four times?" To which me mate's dad replied, "Well, I need four of yours to get one of Alex Young's ..." His brother-in-law was absolutely mortified, but St John burst out in hysterics. Classic. How I wish I was there. **Paul, Bootle (10/05/04)**

THE KANCHELSKIS DERBY was beamed back to Goodison – my mate couldn't get an Anfield ticket so watched it there. When they went 2-0 down some disaffected Red stood up and shouted "Can't you change the fucking channel on that thing? Baywatch is on the other side." To which a Blue replied without missing a beat, "Yeah, more tits in red." There is us and there is them. **Willow (16/02/02)**

WE WERE WATCHIN' EVERTON against the Shite on the big screen at Goodison, when Davie Weir snaps Smicer from behind. When Smicer gets up, sum fella from behind us shouts, "That's a fuckin' disgrace, Davie, the twat got back up." Sheer class. **Mitch 'The Toffee' Murphy (23/08/02)**

AT THE DERBY MATCH, back in '93 – where Billy Kenny arrived as quickly as he vanished. I was sitting in the Gwladys Street with me old fella. When Liverpool took the lead, three Redshites stood up and started singing and turning to the rest of the stands. Minutes later, Mo Johnson equalised and then Beardo scored that cracking winner. After the Blue hordes had slightly quietened down, me old fella shouts, "Where've the Beverley Sisters gone?" Cue general laughter and the slumped shoulders and further depressed air of the Redshites. "Oh, I never felt more like singin' the Blues, when Everton win and Liverpool lose." **BlueForEver (18/01/02)**

AFTER THE WEST BROM GAME this season some fella in the pub on the Saturday night after watching the footy on ITV shouted, "What a bargain – twenty-four quid for a ticket, ten quid for a hat, two fifty for a programme, but watching the Kopites' faces when that twat Dudek dropped another bollock against Fulham – PRICELESS. The pub was in uproar. **John from Breck Road (02/12/02)**

IN THE 1992 'PETER BEARDSLEY' DERBY at Goodison – what a day! Sky was still relatively new. You may remember the 'Sky Strikers' and the fireworks at full time? Well, at half-time they had inflatable Everton and Liverpool sumo wrestlers in the semi-circle. Cue some arl fella: "Aye, aye, they're bringing Jan Molby on." **Duncan Disorderly (24/11/02)**

NOT REALLY A SHOUT but a funny comment. Outside Goodison in the early 60s getting Jimmy Tarbuck's (!) autograph. As he's signing, he says, "I shouldn't really be here, I'm a Liverpudlian." Quick as a flash me Dad says, "Don't worry – he only wants it for a swap." Exit Tarby severely pissed off. Never knew me Dad had it in him. **Rob (19/11/02)**

DERBY GAME AT GOODISON, half-time, massive queue for the gents, one RS pipes up. "You don't have to queue up for a piss at Anfield." Fella next to me replies in a flash, "Yeah, but you all sit down to piss over there." **HM (20/02/02)**

WE WERE AT THIS PRESS CONFERENCE the other day and this French bloke with big, boggle eyes said, "We have turned the corner." Well, we all fell about laughing. **Robbie Rae (18/02/03)**

HESKEY ROLLING ROUND ON THE FLOOR again after being run over by Dunne, "Never mind the stretcher, just get a fucking shovel." **Blue Willo (04/10/01)**

MANY YEARS AGO when we were on the Kop for a derby match, a Redshite was waving a big brass bell. A Blue shouted to him, "Eh, mate, sell your pies and fuck off home." **David Evans (30/12/03)**

AT THE DERBY MATCH this season against the Redshite, their number 7 was warming up before the game right next to the Park End where I sit. I jumped up and shouted (at the top of my voice), "Oi! Smicer! YOU ARE SHITE!" and sat back down with a smug grin on my face. Some 8-year-old kid then taps me on the shoulder and says, "Hey, mate, that's not Smicer, it's Kewell." Needless to say, I said fuck all for the rest of the game, I was too embarrassed. **Lee Flaherty (13/12/03)**

DERBY AT ANFIELD, another 0-0. Babb gets booked and my mate shouts, "The ref's writing BABB and you know it's not his A Level results." Top shout. **Jeff Hanlon (11/08/02)**

THIS YEAR AT THE WHITEWASH WIN at Goodison over the Shite, a fella stood up in the middle of the Gwladys and shouted, "Oh Liver Liver!" at this point everyone was ready to jump on him. He continued, " Liver, Liver, Liver, Liver sausage and mash" and sat down. The whole section erupted in laughter. Great day! **Big Admhez (18/01/05)**

AT LEEDS THE OTHER WEEK. The Leeds fans all round the ground starting chanting, "Same old Fowler, always scoring." As if by magic every Blue joined in, "Same old Fowler, always snorting." Quality. **Paul McComb (02/01/02)**

THE FUNNIEST THING that I ever heard was at the end of the Shite v Sunderland game, when Reid shouted to Tommo, "Fuck off you, big nose." See, it is not only us that knew about the conk from Kirkby. **Martin Tiesteel (14/01/02)**

PICTURE THE SCENE AT ANFIELD in 1995/1996 when Kanchelskis scored 2, three of us were in the Kop, singin' and dancin' away a few minutes after we went 2-0 up. One Kopite twat turned round and said, "Fuck off, you bitter Blues, when was the last time you scored two at Anfield?" Me mate replied straightaway, "About five minutes ago, you twat!" Classic. **Michael Berrill (30/12/01)**

AFTER THE DERBY at the Shite's ground this year, Blue standing in Anfield Road shouting to the Red Noses pointing in the direction of Priory Road. "Passport control and coaches to Devon this way." Top Shout. **Davey Blue (29/04/02)**